W9-BJV-506

WILLIAM BYRD OF WESTOVER

WByrd

WILLIAM BYRD OF WESTOVER

BY

RICHMOND CROOM BEATTY

With Illustrations

Boston and New York

HOUGHTON MIFFLIN COMPANY

The Riverside Press Cambridge

1932

PS
724
A6
B42

COPYRIGHT, 1932, BY RICHMOND C. BEATTY

ALL RIGHTS RESERVED INCLUDING THE RIGHT TO REPRODUCE
THIS BOOK OR PARTS THEREOF IN ANY FORM

The Riverside Press
CAMBRIDGE · MASSACHUSETTS
PRINTED IN THE U.S.A.

TO
FLOY

33699

NOTE

I SHOULD like to thank the following gentlemen for their sympathetic help in the writing of this biography: Drs. Edwin Mims, Walter Clyde Curry, and Frank Owsley, and Mr. Edd. Winfield Parks, of Vanderbilt University; Mr. E. Sydnor Ownbey, of Birmingham Southern College; and Mr. J. Tyree Fain, of the University of Illinois.

I am also indebted to Mr. W. G. Stanard, of the Virginia Historical Society, and to Mr. I. R. McIlwaine, of the Virginia State Library, for generous assistance during my stay in Richmond; and to Mr. William Byrd, of New York City, for permission to use the Kneller portrait.

Dr. John Donald Wade, of Vanderbilt University, first interested me in Byrd. Always, no matter how pressed, he had time to talk over its progress with me, to read the chapters as they were first written, to read them again as they were revised. What of merit one may find in the work represents, I dare say, faint echoes of his wisdom. My regret is that these echoes are not plainer, that the mirror in which he sees himself reflected lacked the polish to give back a just image.

R. C. B.

MEMPHIS, TENNESSEE
November, 1931

CONTENTS

ILLUSTRATIONS

INTRODUCTION

I

THE biographer who chooses to write about early Virginia Cavaliers is faced with a situation not wholly prepossessing. Usually, he finds a deplorable absence of data regarding the slight but revealing incidents in the daily lives of his subjects. Their gossip over teacups, their domestic blisses or miseries, their whims, what they said to visiting friends — all the small but pleasant talk that gives individuality to character — is not to be known. For these gentlemen were, quite as they should have been, vastly more concerned with living itself than with leaving written records of life. The latter was a task, so they thought, becoming rather the genius of a later and more cloistered generation, a paler generation, such as, perhaps, our own...

But this truly depressing state of affairs left to the fictionist an unsullied field. Colonial Virginia and, to more recent writers, *ante-bellum* Virginia came to mean a mellow, far-off, golden era, from which their own age had fallen somehow into the portion of weeds and outworn faces. What an impeccable sense of honor these former gallants had, what flowing curls tumbled carelessly about their shoulders, how lightly they danced, and with what ravishing ladies — and yet how courageous in war! For the last century, it seems, generation has followed generation, each viewing a no doubt glamorous past with its own particular condoning eyes, reënforcing always in literature what in plain terms might be called the grand Virginia Tradition.

Many an author, in a more general sense, has felt this nostalgia for a South that cannot be again and dedicated to it his printed modicum of devotion. The impulse was one of the inevitable reactions to the wretchedness that followed 1865, assuming at that time the proportions of a movement. Plainly, an introduction is no place for even a muster of names. But some attention to the leaders of this group who have tended to idealize early Virginia is demanded, for reasons shortly to appear, if one is to fit a life of Byrd properly into the scheme of things.

The line of succession is long and distinguished. It began with emphasis when John Pendleton Kennedy, disciple of the romantic Irving, published *Swallow Barn* in 1832. Here was the glamorous, century-old brick mansion with its ornate approaches, its wings, its doors, its spacious rooms, its antique furniture. Here, too, was the ever-gracious head of the house, Frank Merryweather, drinking his iced toddy an hour before dinner, his iced wine following dessert, boasting of his horses, discoursing of politics, radiating a ubiquitous hospitality that 'knew no retiring ebb.' The book was Kennedy's defense of an older provincialism which had flourished before his own age of uniformity. 'The country,' he lamented, 'now apes the city in what is supposed to be the elegancies of life, the city in turn adopting what elegancies it can afford to import from across the Atlantic.' The old order was changing, making room for something definitely inferior. Kennedy meant to do this transition no honor.

A second romancer, William A. Carruthers, followed Kennedy by two years with *The Cavaliers of Virginia*. He wrote in stilted fashion. He employed such hackneyed plot devices as mysterious courtships, midnight parleys, prophetic dreams, and weird figures, but for all that he glorified the men and women of the colony's earlier days. That noble rebel Nathaniel Bacon, Virginia Fairfax, Robert Beverley, Governor Berkeley himself — these were the real founders of Old Dominion aristocracy, 'the immediate ancestors of that reckless race of men of so distinct a character, wherever seen.' Carruthers sets forth in bright perspective the home life, the ball and reception at the Governor's mansion, the fox hunt led by Berkeley himself, and a duel between Bacon and Beverley.

John Esten Cooke read all this in his boyhood. He also read Scott and Cooper and Irving. In 1854 these several experiences merged in the form of two works, *Leatherstocking and Silk* and *The Virginia Comedians*, that did much to augment the tradition. Even in the former story, with its border setting and characters of Dutch names, one meets the types Cooke most delighted in drawing: 'elegantly dressed ladies, radiant with rich flowing lace, supporting curiously fashioned towers of hair on white foreheads, and gracefully attentive gentlemen with powdered locks, stiff collared coats, silk stockings and knee breeches.'

The Virginia Comedians was Cooke's masterpiece: Young George Washington pauses to survey the maidens as well as the land of the Earl of Fairfax. Indian raids recall *The Last of the Mohicans*. The bluff old head of Effingham Hall fulminates with truly aristocratic vehemence: 'Every man a vote! Who speaks of it? Who broaches such an absurdity?'

And there is the eldest son of this gentleman, back from

the grand tour, familiar with all forms of dissipation, morally bored with the colony. He dashes books to the floor, kicks dogs, and deports himself as a blood of temper ought, finally running off forcibly with a young actress. Later, he shoots her and wounds her lover and leaves the Dominion until his rashness has blown over. Other types are added to the picture — the parson and schoolmaster, the negro, people of frankly unaristocratic pretensions. Cooke was seeking to present a cross-section of 1765 colonial society.

With Dr. George Bagby's *The Old Virginia Gentleman* (1884), one comes upon a man who wrote of the past in a sort of vehement religious ecstasy. Page called him 'not a fictionist, but a realist,' chiefly, perhaps, because he delighted in recalling the more homely aspects of plantation life — plowing, 'niggers,' the domestic bustle, the endless coming and going of visitors. Pretty cousins, 'the invention of the de'il,' disport themselves saucily through his pages. The head of the establishment is reverent and honest. And as for womanhood, Bagby proclaims to the shiftless youth of his day, 'Hold off, sir, stand back, lay not so much as a finger tip upon her. She is sacred.' Rather, he advises, should he 'inhale the perfume of her breath and hair that puts the violets of the woods to shame. And when you [now ruled by honor] press your first kiss upon the trembling petals of her lips, you shall hear, with ears you knew not you had, the silver chiming of your wedding bells, far up in the heavens.'

But it was left for Thomas Nelson Page to write what one commentator has called 'the epitaph of a civilization.' Surely no one else (as did Page in *In Old Virginia*) has maintained so passionately the thesis of departed glory. Perhaps his major contribution to the tradition lies in his picture of the kindliness of race relations. In 'Marse Chan' he lets an old negro tell the story of his gallant young master, of his duels, his love for the daughter of a political enemy, and how he was brought home dead from the war. Appomattox, to Page, meant the end of a world — a world whose beauty and congenial completeness was never to come again.

The transition from Page to Ellen Glasgow, Cabell, and Hergesheimer is one that calls out definitely current attitudes toward the now firmly established tradition. If Miss Glasgow's social philosophy, as reflected in *Battleground* and *One Man in his Time*, were to be phrased, it would likely assume the outlines of a doctrine that Page would have found distressing to hear. She wrote of Virginia life before and after the war, contrasting conservative and progressive attitudes, and in effect she asked men to look forward, not behind: Washington and Jefferson, your greatly honored colonial archetypes, were not reminiscent, brooding men, but pioneers who faced the future without misgivings. The Old South is a place to which we should go for renewed strength and courage to press on. What has followed 1865 has not been as elegant, as grandly languid, fragrant and dreamlike as what went before; but though more crude it is, for the greater part, better. Miss Glasgow considers the past with clear eyes and is yet hopefully romantic.

With Cabell the social element is less apparent. Of course, one is constantly told, this Virginia gentleman is himself forever escaping reality, now behind an 'evasive idealism' to lands beyond the moon, now in a bitterly romantic symbolism to other places even more frankly imaginative. One nourished upon this dogma finds *The Rivet in Grandfather's Neck* puzzling. Here, for example, is Colonel Rudolph Musgrave, an old Virginia man of honor, settled in the sleepy hamlet of Lichfield, a genealogist whose notion of a sensible morning prayer, declares his wife, is 'God keep us all respectable.' The rivet that prevents him ever from outraging convention is that of tradition, with its innumerable claims and disciplines.

There is a novelist in the book, John Charteris, who writes of life in Lichfield before the war. But for all this, the author makes him out a rather silly and undignified person, who tried to run away with Rudolph's young wife, and who finally was shot by another suspicious husband. Cabell's sympathies throughout are plainly with Colonel Musgrave and the living things he stands for. But in noting this, one is reminded that the young wife Patricia is also sympathetically drawn, though she rather scorns Rudolph's idealism. The most, in brief, that can be said of Cabell is that, while he has busied himself mostly with symbolism, he has written at least one quietly beautiful and vivid book about a Virginian of the old tradition, very much as a portrait painter might pause once to do a sunset.

Something like this might be inferred of Hergesheimer. In *Balisand*, his story of Richard Bale, who had fought with Washington and who clung to older aristocratic pretensions in face of the rising tide of Jeffersonian ideals, to the memory of an old love, and to the home of his fathers, is objectively told throughout. It seems, thus, that with these later romancers even the shadow of purposiveness had faded, that they have come simply to see a leisurely beauty in the Virginia of an earlier day and have sought to capture it in beautiful prose.

2

It is plain what relation ought to exist between this imposing bulk of fact and semi-legend and a biography of a man largely contemporary with the period it so exalts. A life of William Byrd should, I think, faithfully picture a long idealized type. It ought to tender a different eminence from which one interested in such intangibles may, if he chooses, consider respective Reality and Myth. Above all, it ought not to neglect the more unfortunate side of colonial existence, out of deference to the fact that the romantic legend has largely ignored this aspect altogether.

Virginia lavished its possible gifts upon Byrd in gracious abundance. It made him its spokesman many a time in England. It granted him land in extravagant quantities. It took him into its counciliar deliberations. He was one of its nobility. But there were other less tangible though quite as important necessities that neither Virginia nor any other new-world atmosphere ever could hope to furnish him. The complete spiritual satisfaction his nature required, that oneness with older cultural traditions, was innately foreign to the land of his birth. Byrd had absorbed this desire in his childhood, but he absorbed it in England, and England was not his home.

It was well that he could content himself in some measure

with prophesying events to be fulfilled thereafter: war with France, the expulsion of the Spanish, the colonial independence movement, the emancipation of slaves. These things assuaged the bitterness of his longing. About his duties as plantation owner, as venerable member of His Majesty's Council, he was able to go with a mellow gentility — 'a well-bred gentleman and polite companion,' to quote his epitaph, 'with a great elegance of taste and life.' But to learn the grace of it entailed much self-discipline, much more surrender.

To many it appears almost a sacrilege to intimate, further, that the Virginians' economic system left something, perhaps a great deal, to be wished for; that for all the grandeur of that languid civilization, its great men were bludgeoned, then as now, by the most petty of all considerations; that a shortage of so despicable a thing as money could lend a note, not alien to tragedy, to the most genial of dispositions, in the most engaging of companions. Such facts as this the romancers have not dwelt on, and wisely, for the stuff of romance is not in it. And yet it told largely upon the characters of these men of early Virginia. If Byrd's life is typical, it told so largely, in fact, that one is almost bewildered at the complacency with which, in face of it, he held as always to the ideals of his past — the unquestioned presuppositions of his existence. There were times in his life that might well have driven less settled spirits to flaming anger, to futile protest, or to all spiritual renunciation.

But in Byrd these emotions were dormant. He cried out, it is true — Who in any age can escape crying out? — but he went no further. Life in its conventional aspects beamed down upon him as a settled, bulky, static something the outlines of which one accepted unthinkingly. If it wrought evilly, one had one's wit to oppose to it. And if one's wit, for all its nimbleness, proved inadequate, why, then one was beaten, and that was the last of it. One took things as they were. One never revolted. Revolt did not come until 1776, and William Byrd's son was not among its leaders.

WILLIAM BYRD OF WESTOVER

I

SCION OF PROMISE

Let, therefore, this child of three, fresh from the green serenity of England, find for once his own fields greener and more serene on his return. Let him spend a few brief years in a delight unalloyed by remembrances of another land. Let Virginia for once be home for him. All this must pass. . . .

THE offer, say what one would, deserved attention.

William Byrd, age eighteen, son of a goldsmith, child of fortune, gazed out into the murkiness of London and considered the letter before him. Uncle Stagg, from his place up the James River in Virginia,[1] had written it two months before. The old gentleman felt lonely, it was plain. For years and years he had wanted children. One needed them in the new world, be he wealthy or poor, aristocrat or struggling yeoman. But in this case the blessing had been denied. 'Come over and I'll make you my heir,' young Byrd's kinsman was saying!

Leave London in 1670? Why, what a jolly place the town was becoming, now with Cromwell dead eleven years, and the Puritans silent, and King Charles, God save him! in all his kingly glory on the throne! And women were acting in the latest comedies of Mr. Wycherley and of the new laureate, Mr. Dryden. What a stir Nell Gwyn was making, even with His Majesty himself! And surely since Mr. Wren began his work on the public buildings no other city in the world could rival this one for sheer beauty. Streets were wider, houses new, plainly there could never again be a plague or a fire as devastating as the last one of four years ago. Leave all this, and his father's jewelry business, soon to fall to him, for a plantation somewhere across the treacherous Atlantic?

But there was another side to the picture, and the youth, because he was more sober than otherwise, considered it more profoundly. Assume he were to stay on in England. There would be the glamour his mind had dwelt on. There would be tolerable economic success. Possibly political prestige might come also, for the labor guilds were powerful, ruling the city.[2] He would wed another busy tradesman's daughter, and a large family would follow, no doubt.

Yet something which made these prudential virtues strangely unsatisfying had come into the Byrd character at this lad's birth. For Grace Stagg, his mother, was of a family of more ambitious pretensions — a family one of whose scions had years ago broken with British provincialism and established himself as a power in Virginia. A pioneering merchant he had been, able to flatter Puritan when Puritan was in the saddle, but able also to appease the King upon his return from exile at Breda.[3] This desire to ride the winds to true eminence had passed from his grandfather Stagg to young Byrd.

The son of this grandfather, Uncle Stagg, doubtless suspected as much. Doubtless, by way of enticement, he wrote of his own influence with the colony's Governor, doubtless he mentioned his holding the office of Auditor-General, doubtless he told of his seat in the Council.[4] And doubtless, as young Byrd weighed the larger implications of these facts — position, wealth, dignity, acres and acres of land — and thought, on the other hand, of how his father and his father's father had struggled through their aimless lives amid the tragic obscurity of caste-bound London — doubtless when he pondered these things, and the proffered opportunity of escape, he forgot the gayety of his city completely, and remembered only that he was young and that Life and Adventure stretched cleanly before him.

The ship that brought Byrd over in the autumn of 1670 sailed up the James until it could sail no farther, stopped by the falls. A little way from a wharf on the left bank (in what is now Richmond, on the Manchester side of the River) [5] stood a stone house of two stories, singularly imposing, singularly surprising amid so many miles of virgin wilderness. It graced the foreground of an eighteen-hundred-acre plantation. The youth landed here with all his goods: a seaman's chest filled with clothes, a few books.

And Uncle Stagg, who greeted him, was true to his word. Childless he had lived, childless the next year he died. And at his death the goldsmith's son came into his inheritance.

A vast deal of sound advice was given him, along with the property. In the will he was cautioned, among other things, 'not to be led away by the evil instructions he shall receive from others, but to be governed by the prudent and provident counsel of his aunt, the testator's loving wife.' [6]

'Not to be led away by evil instructions.' One suspects that Byrd never forgot that phrase. His life, except for his grand adventure into Virginia, appears uniformly sober and industrious. And it was much the same precept that he passed on to his distinguished son. 'Above all things,' he wrote him when *he* was nineteen, 'be mindful of your duty to heaven and then, you may be assured, God will bless you in all your undertakings.' [7]

Byrd found that life in the colony justified his most extravagant hopes. His uncle had not died before securing Governor Berkeley's interest in his behalf. He was everywhere recognized as a rising young man of property and influence, in line, when he had matured somewhat, for the Receiver-Generalship and for a seat in the Council. Meanwhile, he busied himself with looking after his tobacco plantations, with enlarging the profitable Indian trade Stagg had begun, and with strengthening his friendships and general social position.

This latter consideration led to his marriage. One needed a wife on the frontier, a wife who could manage negroes, and the countless other domestic duties of an estate. One needed also to marry into a family of genealogical prominence; a lapse in this regard would be politically unwise. The wedding occurred in 1673. The bride was Mary Horsemanden, age twenty-one, left a widow three years before by the death of her first husband.[8]

With this union the Byrd line, dating back to Hugo le Brid's arrival with the Conqueror in 1066,[9] identified itself with another at once older and far more distinguished. For the ultimate sire of this house was the Holy Roman Emperor Charlemagne.[10] Its imposing ancestry proceeds from him through six kings of France, three emperors of the East, two rulers of Naples and one of Hungary down to Edward III of England. Thence, John Duke of Lancaster is followed by four English lords. The name Horsemanden itself first appears in the person of Thomas Horsemanden, who was rector of the church at Purleigh, Essex, from 1624 until his death eight years later.[11] It was the nephew of this gentleman, Colonel Warham Horsemanden, who found the triumph of the Puritans so disagreeable that he came to live in Virginia.[12]

He settled in Charles City County, a popular and typical Cavalier. In a few years he was appointed to the Council. But Virginia, for all this distinction, was not England, and with the Restoration he sailed again for Kent. Later he moved back to the old family seat at Purleigh and, like his grandfather, became patron of the church there. He was a kindly gentleman of no little consequence, one who had seen more than his share of the droll inconsistencies of this world. The leisure of his declining years he dedicated, appropriately, to educating the grandchildren sent him from Virginia.

The oldest of these grandchildren, William Byrd II, son of William Byrd and Mary Horsemanden, author and otherwise man of parts, was born March 28, 1674, in the house Stagg left his father.[13]

Life for this favored youngster began with an adventure. Adventure, not to say considerable danger, indeed was in the air. For that eloquent rebel, Nathaniel Bacon, whose plantation lay near Byrd's, was definitely at odds with His Majesty's Governor, planning an attack against the Indians without that Governor's consent.

Under the circumstances, one could scarcely blame him. The powerful Susquehannas were on the warpath again, making bloody forays more and more deeply into forbidden territory. On one of them they had raided Bacon's place and slain, among others, his overseer. On another, three of Byrd's servants had been killed. The Byrd household, including his wife and child, was obviously threatened. He sent them both to England, to Father Horsemanden, until the trouble was over.

But when would the handsome Mr. Bacon act, neighbors wondered. Hadn't he said, in one of his inspired moments, that 'if the redskins meddle with me, damn my blood but I'll harry 'em, commission or no commission'? [14] Byrd met Captain James Crews, Henry Isham, Jr., and Bacon to talk the situation over.

Across the river, at a place called Jordan's Point, leaderless militiamen from near-by counties were slowly collecting. The alarm had been general. The four friends watched them gather, freely disposing, meanwhile, of a quantity of rum. Take some over to them, Byrd suggested to Bacon. Shown this favor, they would fight for him without a commission. Bacon hesitated. To lead an attack against a foreign power without being authorized was plainly forbidden. He had long known that. But the rum flowed on, and his overseer, Bacon reflected, had been a man among men, after his own heart. His blood cried out for revenge. Rot the redskins, he would harry 'em. The colonists were fighting to protect their homes. Berkeley knew of the danger, but, safe in Jamestown, he had discredited it and had failed to act. Finally, when his companions agreed to help, Bacon accepted the responsibility, crossed the river, immediately gained the support of the militiamen, and was signally victorious in the ensuing battle. Byrd commanded part of the attack.

After this event, however, the two friends parted company. The next Assembly, sympathetically aroused by the victory, decreed that an effective military force should be raised and that Bacon should command it. This compliment to the young leader pleased Berkeley not at all. Bacon's military action had been wholly unauthorized, and the Assembly's measure went unsigned. Bacon thereupon marched to Jamestown with armed followers and demanded an official commission.[15] Taken thus helpless, the Governor was forced to acquiesce. Yet he waited no longer than was required for his adversary to leave the island before declaring him a traitor and a rebel against the King's government — as, without any doubt, he was.

Bacon's manifesto in reply speaks eloquently for itself:

If to plead the cause of the oppressed, if sincerely to aim at His Majesty's honor and the public good without any reservation or by-interest, if to stand in the gap after so much blood of our dear brethern bought and sold, if after the loss of a great part of His Majesty's colony deserted and dispeopled, freely with our lives and estates to endeavor to save the remainder be treason — God Almighty judge and let the guilty die.[16]

By some strange distortion of poetic justice, Bacon himself died a few weeks later, the victim of a fever contracted while hiding in the swamps. Berkeley, it would seem, regarded the event as the handiwork of God. And by way of assisting Him in so laudable a work, he executed some two score of the young rebel's followers — 'more,' King Charles is reported to have said, 'than I put to death for the murder of my father.'

Needless to say, when Bacon marched to Jamestown, thus arraying himself in direct opposition to the existing government, Byrd was no longer numbered among his followers. In the first Indian raids, upon his own plantation, it had been different. Self-defense was always pardonable. But a young man of Byrd's practical mind drew a sharp distinction between protecting his home and opposing the King's chosen representative. To the grace of God and an uncle's sterility he was indebted for an estate on tidewater James River, and was well in line for a seat in the Council. He had no inclination to jeopardize either through a serious difference with the established order.[17]

Meanwhile, in England, Mrs. Byrd was lauding Bacon's exploits extravagantly. 'Before ever he went out against the Indians,' she related,[18] 'there were said to be about two hundred of the English murdered by the barbarians, and posts came in daily to the governor giving notice of it, and yet no course was taken to secure them 'til Mr. Bacon went out against them.'

She told, also, of the three men her own husband had lost, and of Berkeley's being so possessed to the contrary that he would not believe this fact to be other 'than a mere pretence for to make war, and that these men were only shut up in a chamber to make the world believe they were murdered.'

And probably she told, too, of the precipitate way in which she and her little son had been packed off to sea because of the danger's immediacy. There was something irresistibly romantic in fleeing for one's life, and in telling about it after the peril was past.

By 1677, Virginia was quiet again, and young Will and his mother returned. He completed the first of his five trips to England with only the vaguest notion of what he had seen there. It would not be so the second time, and only a necessity of the bitterest sort, a bludgeoning necessity, would be able to drag him back the third, fourth, and fifth times.

Let, therefore, this child of three, fresh from the green serenity of England, find for once his own fields greener and more serene on his return. Let him spend a few brief years in a delight unalloyed by remembrances of another land. Let Virginia for once be home for him. All this must pass.

But Will Byrd, during the next three years, had no perception of this pending bitterness. Life as lived so close to the frontier was an experience of measureless zest. How many times, for example, must he have ordered his slave or a servant to row him across the river and up to the tall cliff on its north side. It was a fine place to go when one wanted to see a far way! The domestic who looked after him must have been bewildered listening to the many things so small a young fellow seemed to know about:

Today he would be telling of his father's Indian traders, anxious for their return. He knew the place on the other side of the stream where their trail began. He remembered hearing how for more than four hundred miles these hardy bargainers had penetrated the interior wilderness, reaching even the remote Catawbas and another tribe, the Cherokees, who they said lived beyond, far to the south.[19] The times they failed to get home again were not seldom, but when they did, what loads of furs they brought on the backs of their hundred pack-horses! Surely out of a caravan of fifteen men, their usual size,[20] there were always a few who welcomed an opportunity to tell the strange adventures of their journey, especially to an employer's son who seemed so eager to listen. These were the stories his mind first fed on. And possibly from them one may date the beginning of Byrd's constant interest in the colorful strangeness that characterized the backwoods.

Yet by long odds the days of highest importance to Will, and indeed to his father, were those that brought a vessel from England. He was always among the first who sighted it, high mast and swelling sail emerging from behind a bend in the river, close at hand. What a shout he made at the sight! Before the captain had managed to anchor, the plantation wharf would be lined with servants, slaves, their master, and his son. And on the porch of the house near by Mrs. Byrd, too, stood, her second child in her arms, awaiting anxiously what letters the ship's commander had brought from home.

After unloading their cargoes of such freight as duffles, window glass, cotton goods, and the like — or rum and sugar if they had stopped by the Barbadoes [21] — these grizzled, half-starved sailors would be ordered to roll down Byrd's five-hundred-pound hogsheads of tobacco and place them aboard ship. It was great to watch them, cursing at their tedious labor, or to listen to the captain's stories of pirates barely avoided on the trip over, and how these villains literally clustered about the two capes near the river's mouth.

But an event like this one did not come often. Meanwhile, young Byrd had had another birthday. He was seven years old; the time for the beginning of a long honored process was at hand.

Will's father could not choose but send him to England for an education — could not, that is, if he would have him mature a gentleman. The boy had already learned to read and write at home, but even a Cavalier mother could find no leisure to teach anything more amid the 'great family of negroes' at the plantation.

Of course there were the field schools in the colony itself. Clergymen held them at centrally located homes, and a lad living some distance away might board nearer by. But these uncertain, makeshift sessions could not carry an ambitious student very far.

Free schools, with two negligible exceptions,[22] were unheard of. Governor Berkeley had well summarized the colony's educational status when, in 1671, he answered certain questions for the Lords of Trade:

'I thank God,' he replied to one query, 'that there are no free schools or printing; for learning has brought disobedience, and heresy, and sects into the world, and printing has divulged them, and libels against the best government. God keep us from both.'[23]

Yet Byrd's father, now called 'Esquire' and holding a seat in the Council,[24] would probably have sent him abroad, even had Virginia schools been all schools then were supposed to be. For classroom exercises, he was not slow to perceive, were only a few of many things that a youth of the colony would need to know when his time came for playing the man. He would need graces to win a ruler's favor, the *savoir-faire* born of rich experience. And possibly Byrd felt this thing also: that to bring up a child in Virginia at this date without an intimacy with an older culture, unaware through personal experience of what a spiritually and socially full life meant, was a heartless, Philistine thing to do. And doubtless he reflected, too, with

SALEM COLLEGE LIBRARY
Winston-Salem, North Carolina

a pride born of pardonable tenderness, that the amenities of London, which he had seen only externally, on holiday occasions, could be enjoyed by his son as a matter of course.

Will reached England sometime in 1681. He was sent to Father Horsemanden, at Purleigh, who in turn placed him under one Christopher Glassock. In 1685 his father received from this gentleman the gratifying news that the boy was learning rapidly.

This was a trait that never left him. William Byrd II was a student all his life, keeping up with the scientific world of London when few of his countrymen were aware of its existence.[25] One suspects that he acquired his scholarly instincts in childhood. 'Never let it be said,' he admonished his own godson as an old man, 'that your back is forced to suffer for the defects of your head. And if you should ever come to ride the still horse, don't let it be on account of your book, but for some sprightly action, or gaiety of heart.'[26]

With the elder Byrd becoming more and more prominent as trader, planter, and as a man of political influence in the colony, it was natural for him to desire that his son and successor be able to maintain the position he would eventually inherit. This fact probably induced him in 1689 to send Will to Holland, for nowhere could one learn more about the sordid intricacies of late seventeenth-century trade than from the Dutch, whose mastery of the subject was rarely disputed.

But Will did not profit by the change. The people about him were too completely foreign, and within a year he was tired of them and had asked to be taken away. His father

The place was aristocratic from the beginning. For-
tescue in the late fifteenth century notes that by reason
of its great expense 'the sons of gentlemen only do study
the law in the Temple.' [3] According to Shakespeare, it
was in the Temple garden overlooking the Thames that
the rival houses of York and Lancaster adopted their red
and white insignias in a dispute which precipitated the
thirty-year War of the Roses:

> This brawl today
> Grown to this faction in the Temple garden
> Shall send, between the red rose and the white,
> A thousand souls to death and deadly night.[4]

Men of undisputed high place in English literature had
studied there before Byrd. It seems likely that the prominence of such esteemed alumni as Raleigh, Thomas Over-
bury, Beaumont, John Ford, Evelyn, Shadwell, Southerne,
Congreve, and Rowe encouraged his earliest inclinations
to write. Oldmixon, whose first edition of *The British
Empire in America* was published in 1708, speaks of a
manuscript history of Virginia, 'written with a great deal
of spirit and judgment by a gentleman of the province, to
whom this writer [Oldmixon] confesses he is very much
indebted. I refer to the History of Virginia by Colonel
Byrd, whom I knew when I was in the Temple, and the
performance answered the just expectation I had of that
gentleman's ability and exactness.' [5]

The routine of entrance into the Temple was simple,
provided a candidate's family had influence. To a brief
application Byrd attached an endorsement by two prac-
ticing barrister alumni and a matriculation fee of forty

pounds. These gentlemen were supposed previously to have examined him on his general knowledge of the classics. The object of their questionings, explains John Wyatt, 'was not to ascertain whether a student was a good scholar or not, but to see how he spent his time and whether he was of gentlemanly habits, so that we might have some security for his being fit to come into such a society.' [6] The only other preliminary to admittance consisted in a deposit of one hundred pounds, which, with singular appropriateness, was returned to the student after he had been called to the bar and was ready to begin practice.

Byrd was allowed to do rather as he pleased the three years he spent in the Temple. To stay in the good graces of his instructors, or Benchers, as they were called, it was only necessary to dine in the hall three times during each quarter. This rule had been passed with the idea of making one's character known to his fellows.[7] In short, masters of the Inns of Court of Byrd's day were interested quite as much in a member's social graces and integrity as they were in his ability to plead a case; and according to at least one authority,[8] the Templars succeeded in distinguishing themselves for gallantry as well as for their legal lore. But actual training was available if desired.

Before Byrd completed his course, for example, he had been compelled to prepare and plead cases no less than twelve different times, to the satisfaction of the Bencher who had been assigned to him as tutor.[9] It was only upon this gentleman's recommendation that he could have come before the committee who formally called him to the bar, April 12, 1695.

Byrd was most strongly attracted by the social life of the Temple. Since the beginning of the Elizabethan stage the four Inns of Court had been associated with its drama. Sackville and Norton, two Inner Temple barristers, had presented before Elizabeth the first English tragedy of *Gorboduc* in January, 1561, the several parts being played by fellow law students.[10] Shakespeare's *Twelfth Night*, if we may believe the diary of one John Manningham of the Middle Temple, was originally performed in Temple Hall on Candlemas Day, 1602. Many of the masques of Beaumont and Fletcher were presented first in the same place, with the King and Queen as interested spectators.

The tradition of gayety thus firmly established suffered little until years after Byrd's death. During his own student days he also found much amusement in the yearly round of entertainments prevalent between All Hallows Eve and Candlemas, an interval of three months. This colorful interim, featured most often by excessive bibacity, had become an essential element in the Templar's academic experience. The custom had been taken over from houses of the nobility in which a 'Lord of Misrule' was appointed to prepare dances, banquets, theatricals, and similar diversions during the same season. The Czar of Muscovy, Peter the Great, attended these Temple revels, in December, 1697, when there was 'a riotous and revelling Christmas, according to usage.' [11]

Among the friendships that made this period one he always remembered pleasantly, Byrd formed three of unusual importance. The earliest was with Sir Robert Southwell, who seems, until his death in 1702, to have taken an unfailing fatherly interest in the boy. With his social influence, Byrd found ready entrance into the most polite and learned circles of London. Among others, Southwell introduced him to Charles Boyle, Earl of Orrery, and until this nobleman died, in 1731, it is doubtful that Byrd had any friend whom he more esteemed. This intimacy he owed to his own personality, rather than to any inherited fortune or position; for compared to the wealth of an English lord, his own was inconsiderable.

Byrd's third association was of a livelier nature. Benjamin Lynde, a fellow student from Salem, Massachusetts, had entered the Temple in 1692. Perhaps it was in the company of this New-Englander that he first visited the French Court. At all events, they had seen London together under conditions not to be lightly dismissed. Lynde became Chief Justice of his colony in 1728, but Byrd was not inclined to let him forget the indiscretions of his youth. In 1735 he wrote him from Westover:

If I could persuade our captain of the guardship to take a cruise to Boston at a proper season, I would come and beat up your quarters at Salem. I want to see what alteration forty years have wrought in you since we used to intrigue together in the Temple. But matrimony has atoned sufficiently for such backslidings, and now I suppose you have so little fellow-feeling left for the naughty jades that you can order them a good whipping without any relenting. But though I should be mistaken, I hope your conscience, with the aid of three score and ten, has gained a complete victory over your constitution, which is almost the case of Sir of,

your obedient humble servant,
W. BYRD [12]

2

When Byrd returned to Virginia, immediately upon receiving his call to the bar, the character of its society was permanently fixed. Experience had rather completely dispelled the illusions of the romantic gentlemen who came to Jamestown in 1609, bringing a perfumer and nine tailors with them. Successive migrations peopled the colony with settlers who, if of humbler and more practical natures, at least were prepared for the exigencies which faced them. 'Few men of high social rank in England established families in Virginia,' says Wertenbaker. 'The leading planters of the seventeenth century were mercantile in instinct and unlike the English aristocrat of the same period.' [13]

But a rapid transformation was inevitable. With a network of navigable waterways, forming, what John Fiske has called the colony, 'a sylvan Venice,' a decentralized economics soon developed. Scattered along the banks of the Rappahannock, Potomac, and James Rivers there suddenly appeared a series of decidedly feudal estates. Here the slave was gradually replacing indentured labor. Most of the servants thus freed, as well as many new settlers of less prominence, found it difficult to take up desirable tracts of land and were moving on into Carolina. Those who remained soon learned that nothing was able to rival political offices in assuring them a permanent position of influence among their fellows. Membership in the Assembly or the Council they regarded as the acme of achievement, for it was from among the personnel of these houses that various other governmental authorities were chosen.

Young Byrd's father had made the most of this arrangement. In 1687, by virtue of a trip to England for the purpose, he got himself appointed Receiver-General of the King's revenue. Thus (in addition to being a Councillor and, through that office, as shall be seen later, a Justice in the colony's Supreme Court), he became the collector of all quit-rents, or taxes, and at the same time the auditor of all accounts, including his own. It was a highly convenient situation and one in which, had Byrd desired, he could have practiced the grossest fraud. His books were not examined with any attention until two years after his death.[14]

Cavalier graces in the Old Dominion flourished beside virulent survivals of puritanism. Aristocrats raced their horses for large stakes. When the payment of wagers was grudged, the affair went to court. Often, if unable to reach a decision, the jury would be confined 'without bread, drink, candle, or fire'[15] until its members felt differently disposed. Ducking-stools stood near the race-tracks, at convenient bodies of water. They were used to rebuke witches convicted of riding their neighbors nightly about the countryside. Stocks might be seen at any settlement.[16]

But these last two disciplinary agents were designed for the lower class. No gentleman of breeding was exposed to any such ridicule. The latter were often men of 'King' Carter's stamp — high-handed, arrogant transcripts of the eighteenth-century coffee-house 'blood.' Complaints of the yeomen against officials of this type are scattered throughout the records of the time.[17] The truth is, that life in Virginia, from the beginning of its settlement, revealed a tendency to solidify quickly into distinct economic and social strata. In short, life in the colony began at once to parallel conditions in England. The immeasurable advantage in the case of Byrd's father lay in this: through reasons already noted, he was able to move almost at once from the English middle class into the Virginia aristocracy.

And what faith these colonists had in the existing order! 'On the fifteenth day of every October,' wrote George Jordan of Surrey County, in his will, 'there shall be a sermon of mortality preached in my house, it being the day my daughter Fortune Hunt died, and whosoever shall enjoy my land, although it be a thousand generations hence, shall perform this sermon and prayer.' [18]

A thousand generations hence, in memory of his daughter Fortune, and because they were enjoying his land...

And Robert Beverley, with great deliberation, refused to sell three thousand acres fronting the Rappahannock, in spite of a profit of something close to one thousand per cent, 'because,' as the otherwise ready purchaser declared, 'he would not dispose of it as commonly land is disposed of, but would have the deeds made to me for 999 years, which I would not consent to, but insisted on having it for me and my heirs forever.' [19] The Beverleys of the year 2714 would have a great time reclaiming their three thousand acres, old Robert must have thought. And, indeed, it would have been so, though for reasons he hardly suspected.

William Byrd II was never a victim of the delusions of grandeur which obsessed the Carters, or his own brother-in-law, Robert Beverley. As he grew older, it became all too plain that it was his English friends, Boyle, Egmont, and the Southwells, who had the reality of which his was, comparatively, the shadow. After all, what did acres upon acres mean when one's pocket was empty, and creditors importunate?

3

The high esteem in which the elder Byrd was held at the time of his son's return simplified the latter's ready entrance into Virginia political life. He served as a Burgess from Henrico County, the place of his birth, in the session of the Assembly held in September, 1696. His father still owned considerable property there, though he had moved to Westover, some thirty miles farther down the river. But young Byrd evidently found life in Virginia dull. He took advantage of the first opportunity, which offered itself early in 1697, to return to England as a legal representative of the Virginia Assembly. Aided by John Povey,[20] he presented an address of his clients to the Lords of Trade and Plantations sometime during the ensuing summer. Thus he had made but one appearance in the capacity of barrister before he was called upon to oppose that enterprising Scotchman, Mr. Commissary Blair, at the Lambeth Conference in December. In a sense it may be said that the question of higher education in Virginia was dependent upon the outcome of this meeting. And it was a cause that had suffered much.

One interested in assigning to every phenomenon its true source might name Blair the father of higher education in Virginia. Officially, he was the Bishop of London's vicar: As the Governor represented the King, so did Blair the Church. By virtue of this position Blair also held a seat in the Council. It was therefore but natural that the Assembly, when it finally decided to make provisions for a college, should elect Blair to negotiate the business in England. The proposed school was, among other things, to be a training-quarters for divinity students. This, Blair saw at once, would be his prime talking point. Naturally, his prime object was to raise money.

First he visited Attorney-General Seymour. He proposed to this gentleman that part of the colony's taxes be set aside for educational endowment purposes. Two thousand pounds was the sum asked for. He stressed the spiritual nature of his request.

But England was meanwhile at war, and the Attorney-General finally averred with some impatience that the requested fund was needed for things vastly more material than those his visitor had suggested.

'But,' Mr. Blair retorted, 'the people of Virginia have souls to be saved as well as the people of England.'

'Souls?' exclaimed Seymour. 'Souls? Damn your souls! Make tobacco.' [21]

Yet this gruff old Britisher saw the light before Blair had done with him and willingly approved the disbursement.

The zealous Scotchman was likewise active in other quarters. He learned that Robert Boyle, father of Byrd's friend the Earl of Orrery, had provided in his will that four thousand pounds of his estate should be employed in certain 'pious and charitable uses.' Neither the character nor the locality of the beneficiary had been mentioned. Blair immediately met Boyle's executor and aroused his interest in the subject of Indian education so far as to induce him to purchase a Yorkshire manor, the Brafferton. The rents of this property, subject to an annual deduction of forty-five pounds for Harvard College and a like amount for the Society for the Propagation of the Gospel in New England, were deeded over to William and Mary. By the terms of this agreement, Blair's school was to keep as many Indian children in meat, drink, washing, clothes, medicine, books, and education, 'from the first beginnings of letters till they should be ready to receive orders and be sent abroad to convert the Indians, as the yearly income of the Brafferton premises would permit.' [22]

While the details of Boyle's endowment were being looked after, Blair managed to secure another donation of a far more striking sort. The Crown, it seems, had made one of its frequent compromises with pirates by announcing that any member of this brotherhood who surrendered himself by a certain date would be forgiven all past transgressions and allowed to keep a part of his treasure. Many took advantage of the offer to make peace with the government, but three who came in after the time limit had expired were arrested and jailed. These unfortunates humbly petitioned the Privy Council for pardon, alleging that when they first heard of the royal proclamation it was too late to reach port by the day appointed.

It was Blair's chance, and he made the most of it. When he learned of the affair, he laid before these gentlemen a no doubt inviting proposition: He would get them released, if they would give three hundred pounds toward the education of Virginia's divinity students. It would be a pleasure, the pirates agreed, to have a hand in so laudable an enterprise. It meant making one's peace with both Church and State in the grandest imaginable manner. And Blair was true to his word, for by order of the Privy Council the prisoners received that share of treasure allotted them by law, minus the amount promised the college in Virginia.[23]

Now Blair had obtained these several endowments in 1693 and 1694. After securing them he went back to Virginia, raised other funds by subscriptions, and, during the next three years, began his school. But he had, unfortunately, made certain political enemies in the meanwhile, one of whom was Governor Andros himself. Andros accused Blair of filling the Church with Scotchmen and of squandering and misapplying funds given the college. That this indictment might be pressed the more forcibly before the Archbishop of Canterbury, who was to hear the case, Andros employed young Byrd as his attorney. It was plain that matters had come to a crisis and that either Blair or the Governor would have to be recalled.

Byrd defended his client bravely enough — there is certainly no denying this fact.[24] As instructed, he charged Blair with filling his pulpits with Scotchmen, to the serious detriment of religious harmony in the colony. He also affirmed that Blair was unfairly receiving one hundred and fifty pounds of the college funds as salary before the roof on its only building had been completed.

But much interrogation and discussion revealed the truth that Blair had nothing to do with these so-called Scotchmen. The Bishop of London had himself appointed them, and three of those especially complained of were really out-and-out Britishers who were merely so unfortunate as to have inherited Scotch names. Further evidence also established the fact that the Assembly itself had given Blair permission to receive the salary in question, since he had found it necessary to resign his church and income in order to carry on the endowment campaign for William and Mary.

Still young Byrd did not give up; though by the time his two principal charges had been completely overthrown, his case was beginning to seem hopeless. At least he could defend the Governor against slander. With this noble resolve in mind, he demanded proof of certain accusations Blair had spread abroad to the effect that Andros was constantly obstructing the interests of the college.

Proof came immediately and in overwhelming abundance. It developed that the Governor had systematically prevented the collection of funds pledged to William and Mary under his predecessor; that he had allowed twenty thousand acres of the school's property to be occupied by settlers without the consent of its board of trustees; and, worst of all, that he had tried most disingenuously to browbeat this same board into declaring him one of its staunch supporters in a record that would be sent his superiors in England.

Further highly incriminating evidence followed, in reply to which Byrd was able to say very little. Andros resented Blair's increasing influence in the colony and wanted him out of the way. The situation was utterly obvious. It was also plain, in the trial itself, that this young attorney of twenty-three years, who was bravely trying to clear the

Governor's good name, had a quite impossible task on his hands. But one may well doubt whether Andros himself could have urged his own case any better. Within the next few months he was recalled.[25]

After the Lambeth Conference, Byrd continued his stay in England. Since the previous October he had been a resident at Lincoln's Inn,[26] and with a father whose prominence was sufficient to keep him employed, life proved agreeable enough. It was quite likely through the elder Byrd's influence that young William found himself, at a salary of probably one hundred pounds for the first two years,[27] known as Agent for Virginia. During this time he took advantage of the opportunity to study the laws of his colony, for the Lambeth affair had rather thoroughly demonstrated that he knew very little about them.

In 1698, for the first time in this new capacity, Byrd appeared before the Lords of Trade and Plantations with a memorial about some French Protestants the King intended settling on the disputed ground between North Carolina and Virginia. As this property was claimed by both provinces, the Crown had decided to dispose of the matter by creating there a new colony, independent of either. The Huguenots were intended to serve as a nucleus for further population.

But Byrd, moved doubtless by his father's owning land in the place he favored, pointed out that the royal intent was highly unreasonable.[28] The land was, for the most part, swampy, being located near that point commonly designated as the 'fog end of North Carolina.' Such an arrangement would afford all the criminals, servants, and slaves of Virginia a haven whereto they could flee the laws of that colony without fear of being brought back to justice. The ideal solution of the question would result from settling these emigrants on the 'upper parts of James River in Virginia.' There they could enjoy an excellent climate and the added protection of a reasonable government. Byrd dismissed the pretensions of North Carolina's proprietors, who were attempting to bring the refugees into their own territory, by saying that 'in a competition betwixt a plantation belonging to ye King and another belonging to proprietors, the first ought always, in duty and by virtue of ye prerogative, to be preferred.'

His agency was at least partly successful. In March, 1699, the King approved of 'divers French Protestant refugees being settled in Virginia,' but 'in Norfolk County,' [29] not 'on the upper parts of James River.' Yet it appears that some actually went to the upper James and founded a place called the Monacan town, in Henrico County.[30] At the request of the Lords of Trade, Byrd gave the leader of these settlers a letter of introduction to his father.[31]

The second task he undertook as Assembly Agent, in 1701–02, was of a much more important nature. Byrd was advanced three hundred pounds by the House of Burgesses that he might prosecute the matter with the leisure it demanded.[32]

Francis Nickelson had replaced Andros as Governor, and it seems that this gentleman soon found himself at odds with the lower house and with half the Council over the question of sending certain requested aid to New York. That colony was at war with the Five Nations and obviously very much in need of assistance. The appeal had

come as an order from the Crown, and as Governor it was
Nickelson's responsibility to see that the Virginians complied with it. Nine hundred pounds and a company of
soldiers had been asked for.

Byrd's father was among the leading Councillors who
opposed this levy. His reasons therefor he communicated
to his son, and the latter drew up an elaborate memorial
to be presented to His Majesty. Should this privilege be
denied him, Byrd was to direct the document to the Lords
of Trade. This body served as the King's advisors in
colonial affairs, and to convince them of the injustice of a
proposal meant, very likely, that it would not be pressed
further.

In the first place, Byrd's complaint set forth, the New
York colonists' appeals for aid had become chronic and
should no longer be humored. For the past ten years no
less than twenty-five hundred pounds had been sent them
by the Virginia government.[33] The basis of their inability
to maintain peace with the Indians Byrd attributed to
their own self-seeking merchants. These men, he said,
were trying to control the entire native beaver and deer-
skin trade, and they had no scruples about making war, so
long as the hope remained of compelling the Five Nations
to sign a treaty granting them the business.

He wished humbly to point out that the frontiers of
Virginia were quite as much exposed as were those of New
York. They were also far less easily defended 'because of
the scattered nature of the population.' It had become a
daily problem how to ensure the protection of the Virginia
coasts and homes against attack. The colony was as weak
in men as it was poor in money, and any proposal such as

the one under consideration would be attended by direst consequences.

For instance, he contended with an oddly unflattering brand of sophistry, suppose that each individual conscripted should be away for three months — a most reasonable estimate. During that time the King would lose twenty pounds sterling in revenue per man taken, because the soldier in question would not be able to 'labor in tobacco,' while absent. This, of course, was above the cost to His Majesty in transportation, pay, and subsistence while in service. At least three times the quota asked for would flee to North Carolina, 'where no men are required,' rather than risk their lives in war. Those who remained to be drafted would be the property-owners. Lacking their guidance, slaves would neglect their duties in the fields, and the yield of tobacco, and in consequence the royal revenue, would be still further diminished. Finally, with the best men in Virginia away, the colony would itself become an easy prey to an enemy. And if it be taken, Maryland must soon fall also, since nearly all foreign trade went by way of the capes between the two provinces.

Young Byrd directed his petition at first to Queen Anne. 'Whereas,' his preamble declared, 'by his late Majesty's command it was recommended to the Assembly to raise nine hundred pounds towards the assistance of New York, the Council of Burgesses, by reason of their poverty and the expenses they must be engaged in for their own defense, finding themselves incapable to raise said sum, did send over a petition to Her Majesty to supersede his commands.' [34]

But he was not allowed an audience with Her Majesty, and the memorial reached the Lords of Trade only after two friends of the Governor had appeared before them in his own behalf. Colonel Robert Quarry had been a witness to several of Nickelson's earlier struggles with the Assembly and was highly in sympathy with him. This gentleman, along with one Diogenes Wright, the Council clerk who had been sent over for the purpose, so prejudiced the Board in the Governor's favor that they would not allow Byrd to see them personally until after his arguments had been delivered in writing and examined.[35]

They then sent for him and asked him pointedly if there were any objections the Assembly had to make against Nickelson. He replied that there were not. Then the chairman informed him (though the practice had been common for at least thirty years) that the act of the Assembly in selecting its own agent was 'an irregular proceeding,' and that in future whatever complaints that body entertained against a royal decree were to be made through the governor,[36] he being the Crown's representative and the proper person to transmit such grievances to England. The Council, for its part in the matter, was also formally rebuked. Its members replied submissively that they did not realize the refractoriness of the policy and would henceforth discontinue it. This acquiescence meant the end of Byrd's agency.

Meanwhile, he had sought another position without success. The death of Wormley in the spring of 1701 had left vacant the office of Secretary of Virginia, and in competition with Edmund Jenings and William Spencer, Byrd applied to the King for an appointment as successor. The petitions of these three were referred to the Lords of Trade for their opinion. Philip Ludwell, a Councillor who had formerly held the place, wrote this board that the records of the office had been suffered to decay and the position itself left in the past to the charge of under-clerks, and that he hoped they would appoint a man who would be willing to reside at Williamsburg and look after the work personally.[37] After receiving this communication the Lords of Trade decided to wait for Governor Nickelson's opinion as to who ought to be selected.

When young Byrd learned that Nickelson's recommendation was to have weight, he realized that his chances of securing the office were poor indeed. He had opposed this gentleman's New York relief measures until both the Queen and the Lords of Trade had practically refused him any further audience. He decided to try bringing the question to some settlement before Nickelson's preferences could be made known. In November, 1701, he accordingly drew up an address to the Lords of Trade, pointing out what ill consequences were attending their delay and urging that the new officer be chosen at once. 'Mr. Nickelson,' he concluded, 'has scarcely distinguished himself in his administration, since he has failed to inform your Lordships of the merit or management of Colonel Jenings.' [38] Jenings, as Wormley's deputy, had executed the office since the latter's death.

The next month the Lords of Trade set forth the merits of all three candidates to the Crown. They avoided all suggestion of preference except, perhaps, for Byrd. 'He,' they declared, 'is a native of Virginia, son of one of the most prominent of His Majesty's subjects in those parts, is a person of good character, unblamable conduct, and known loyalty to His Majesty and his government, and has had the advantage of a liberal education and knowledge of the laws of England and may be very fit to serve His Majesty as he desires.' [39]

But the office was finally granted to Jenings, 'no objections having come either against his capacity or honesty.' According to Culpepper, the appointee was next to the Governor in power.[40] He named all the county clerks and was clerk of the Council himself, *ex-officio*.

This decision proved a keen disappointment to Byrd. Here, when only twenty-eight years old, his chance at prominence had almost come. With the recommendation the Lords of Trade had given him, the thing seemed inevitable even. Yet somehow the Prince's favor had, in the end, been granted another. And the next year, through no fault of his own and in violation of long-established precedent, the Lords of Trade had suddenly deemed it expedient to abolish the office of Assembly Agent and, incidentally, his own position. It was rather depressing.

III

LOVER ELOQUENT

It is to be regretted that a few of their number did not pause to commit some-thing more of these stirring iambics to paper, for as it has happened the five lines just quoted are the only surviving poetry Byrd ever wrote.

I

To go home to Virginia and resume a place of political importance under the still influential guidance of his father was, no doubt, the policy economic prudence suggested to Byrd, after the Lords of Trade had seen fit to abolish his source of income. Besides, it was time to return! Since childhood he had been there but half a year, and friendships among members of a powerful aristocracy, except in few instances, were yet to be made. In addition, the properties that had been so wisely accumulated by his parent, as well as the offices attached to them, were soon to become his own; for he was an only son.

But recently he had failed to secure an appointment that might have made such a return auspicious — a thing suggestive of independent achievement. Now to go back would entail a certain admission of defeat, and, further, the facing in his own territory of a Governor whom he had opposed abroad unsuccessfully and with some bitterness. Byrd was a man who liked few things as he liked having the law, in the form of a King's approving commission, on his side of a question. It gave him such assurance in times of trouble or dispute. But he had not yet been so favored. This was probably one of the reasons for his remaining in

WESTOVER

England, though at considerable expense, and though his father was alone at Westover, and often sick with the gout.

Of course, there were other reasons of an entirely different nature. It would have been strange indeed for a young Templar of such handsome proportions to neglect the company of ladies in what was preëminently a social age. There are no indications that he was ever thus abnormal. Indeed, one might even wonder how this excellent and eligible gentleman avoided the snares of matrimony as long as he did, in view of the really momentous emotion that seized him in the summer of 1703.

The instant your coach drove away, madam [he writes the object of his fervor], my heart felt as if it had been torn up by the very roots, and the rest of my body as if severed limb from limb. I could not have shed a tear, if I might have gained the universe. My grief was too fierce to admit of so vulgar a demonstration. My soul was perfectly put out of tune, my senses were all stunned and my spirits fluttered about my heart in the last confusion. Could I at that time have considered that the only pleasure I had in the world was leaving me, I had hung upon your coach and had been torn in pieces sooner than have suffered myself to be taken from you. May you be diverted while in Ireland, but may you find nothing there to please you.[1]

The letters which follow to Facetia are much more informing. But there is this to be said for them, and for Byrd's character as well: judged by nineteenth-century standards, the tone of parts of his correspondence may seem scandalous or even plainly indecent, and the remark made elsewhere that Byrd was by nature essentially moral may appear, in consequence, inconsistent. But such is by no means the case. One need only recall his contemporary Swift's account of Gulliver's Lilliput experience, or the adventures of Joseph Andrews or of Tom Jones the foundling, to be convinced that a virile humor and a staunch morality were not at all, in the same person, incompatible. The fact is that the eighteenth century suffered from no such all-perverting blight as did the twentieth at the hands of smug Victorianism. Its heritage had been the Elizabethan age, tempered by reason, mellowed by the graces. It was a healthier era than our own.

Healthier, for the simple reason that the whole of life, to a cultivated man of Byrd's day, was rich in tragic and comic interest. His amusement in the saltily facetious had in itself no snickering morbidity. It was, rather, an intellectual delight, the result of hearing the physically coarse recounted with delicate wit. He was never crude, and crude jesting, it will soon be apparent, he heartily and constantly despised. To censure him, therefore, for the breadth of his humor is completely to fail in appreciating the sanity and balance of life in his age.

The summer Byrd was writing to Facetia he spent in London, though nearly everyone else of his circle had deserted the capital for the spas.

I have been a recluse these three weeks [he writes, the third of July], and know very little how our solitary town behaves itself. Here are hardly people enough left to allow sufficient privacy for intrigues and, therefore, since love don't come to action that way, 'tis going to vent itself in marriages. 'Tis whispered as secret among the ladies (and therefore will soon be all over the town) that Sir Roger Mostyn is going to be married to Lady Essex Finch.[2] Poor Phizinini too, they say, to help Sir Christopher's perspiration, is going to make him her husband, and I can but think what greasy doings there will be betwixt 'em in the dog days.

Byrd then proceeds to relate current gossip about a number of the nobility. In most instances his information is of a general sort, and it is uncertain whether he was intimate with the people discussed, or merely an interested near-courtier who found coffee-house conversation spicy enough to be repeated. Scattered throughout this series of letters are references to such fictitiously named characters as Phizinini, Hedeosinda, Owletta, and the like, made in much the same spirit as those to persons of historical prominence. Facetia must have recognized them at once. Thus it seems probable that if Byrd were not a personal friend of many of the titled persons he discusses, at least his social circle was not much below or different from their own.

The picture of Oxford in his third letter is somewhat unorthodox. He had been up to that university to witness 'the Act.' It was an old custom. Formerly it consisted of a number of theses publicly maintained by candidates for degrees, to give evidence of their proficiency. The ceremony took place early in July. Theses would be discussed on Saturday and Monday, and on the Sunday intervening two of the new doctors of divinity preached Act sermons before the faculty and students. In Byrd's day there were certain compensations for these more serious performances. The undergraduates regarded the occasion as one of general license and selected a 'Terrae Filius' and other character survivals of mediæval masques who played practical and frequently questionable jokes upon the graver members of the university or town.[3]

The reason there has been such a distance between this letter and the last [he apologizes] was an expedition I made to the Act

of Oxford. But whether I have no taste left or but one taste, I
was never so little diverted in my life. The Terrae Filius who
was the wag of the place took the liberty to abuse the grave
doctors of the university, but with such ill manners and so little
good wit that I think it was the most detestable lampoon I ever
heard. And to give your Ladyship a sample to prove what I say
I will repeat two famous passages that provoked an intemperate
deal of mirth amongst the tattered gowns and square caps. He
said of one Dr. Smith, mentioning his name, that he was 'a
bachelor in the college, a cuckold at home, and an adulterer
abroad.' Now, madam, I may safely say that there is not a
nymph in Billingsgate that does not in her common conversation
over a barrel of oysters give as smart characters as this, and that
too without the joint inspiration of the top wits of the neighborhood.

This fine gentleman was not content to abuse the learned
pedants after this gross manner, which I could have forgiven
him because it was his own way; but he also did several ladies the
favor to make kind mention of them, and particularly Lady
Price and her daughters, whom he introduced by way of an
advertisement to a gazette in these words:

'Lost or mislaid: a bundle containing a collection of
paint, false hair, patches, pomatum, and false teeth, belonging to the Lady Price and her daughters. Whoever gives
timely notice shall be well rewarded, because the poor
ladies can't stir abroad until their necessary charms are
recovered.'

When I have given you these noble instances of Oxonian
politeness, I suppose you will have no curiosity to hear anything more about it. I was perfectly sick of the confusion and
impertinence of the place, and thought every day a month 'til I
could return hither again to my hermitage.[4]

Sir Stephen Fox [he concludes, in an impressive array of
London social notes] has married a young Shulamite to keep him
warm. She was a companion of his daughter-in-law and wedded
him at half an hour's warning.

The humor in this innocent item is somewhat concealed, unless one remembers that Sir Stephen had recently celebrated his seventy-sixth birthday.

Toward the last of July, London was a dismal place indeed.

Our town [he informs Facetia] is deserted by everything but dust, ill smells, and — what is worse than either — by the ladies of universal gallantry. Nay I'll swear it is so very solitary here that there is hardly any impertinence or scandal left among us. Lord Guilford is coupled to Mrs. Brownlow, and the gods alone can tell what will be produced by the conjunction of so much fat and good humor. Lord Wharton,[5] in his journey to the north, was taken ill at Northampton, but he is likely to recover, and his lady is once more disappointed of being the richest widow in England. Lady Ann Greville is now dying in good earnest, and her spouse, who has a strange excess of wit and good humor, can't forbear expressing more than ordinary satisfaction ever since she has been given over.[6]

In August everybody had gone to Bath, 'that dear place,' he reminds Facetia, 'where I once imagined myself in heaven by your Ladyship's being there. The Queen goes down in a fortnight and a world of people will follow because there is a crowd, but I won't go because I should think it empty.'

Such lines as the above are curious. Who Facetia was there exists no means of determining, and speculation on the point seems plainly idle. It has been suggested that she was imaginary and that Byrd wrote the entire series of letters merely as literary exercises. But this view is hardly in keeping with his character. Byrd was too fully a man of the world to resort to any such fanciful excursions: all of his other writings have a direct basis in personal observation, in fact. Here, also, his point of view — that of the neglected suitor — appears too consistently maintained for pure fiction. Had the object of his correspondence been merely simulated, one thinks, Byrd would have varied his attitude and themes in order to achieve a more rounded perfection at the art.

But the question of identity is quite confusing. The chances are that Byrd at this date knew some hundred or more ladies, almost any one of whom might have captured his unstable enthusiasm for the summer. Yet of all this acquaintance (if one may in humble honesty confess it) not one is definitely known. To guess, therefore, that this or that person — because she is now remembered for other reasons — was the object of his devotion is little short of ludicrous. The historical Facetia, one fears, is alas long since forgotten, together with all too many of the colorful Chloes, and Celias, and Millamants who were her companions. So be it. Byrd's achievement lies in the fact that to one of these cruel but fair enchantresses he has given a lasting, if not quite exemplary, immortality. He was probably the first native American to write to a woman by other than her legal name. And throughout he signed his effusions 'Veramour.'

But Veramour, for all his entreaties, got never a word from the absent Facetia. He implored her to answer, he upbraided her, he coaxed, he scolded (he is still young), he was dumpish, he was petulant.

He was everything, in fact, except definite. Not once did he suggest positively either seeing her again or any mutual interests that might develop thereafter. A reply to his letters was all he desired. Now no one could censure Byrd

for displaying such consummate tact. But the weakness in
such a policy of reserve is plain: a lady interested in an alliance of relative permanence would be induced by it to push
her quest into other and more likely quarters. And this is
doubtless what took Facetia to Ireland.

Yet how sorely did news of her philandering trouble him!
About the middle of August he left London to attend a sort
of house-party. It was while there, he confides to her, that
the generous host became so solicitous as to call him aside
one night to repeat the rumors of several 'scandalous adventures' in which the object of his affections was reported
to have involved herself since leaving the country. Byrd
listened to this vile slander as long as he could. But repres-
sion soon became impossible. Leaping to his feet in a storm
of unbridled fury, 'these words broke like a tempest from
my mouth':

> By heaven and earth and that one God that formed
> This beauteous world, each word you've spoke is false
> And spawned of hell, that cursed forge of lies,
> Where spiteful fiends contrive with pois'nous breath
> To blast the fame of saints they can't corrupt.[7]

'After distracting myself thus in heroics for half an hour,'
he concludes, 'I paused long enough solemnly to renounce
all further friendship with this officious gentleman and took
horse that very night for the city.'

Infrequent stragglers along the highway to London were
doubtless much amazed at the figure of this dashing horse-
man, his lyrical diatribe about a woman's chastity ringing
plainly defiant above his charge's clatter. One regrets that
a few of their number did not pause and commit something
more of these eloquent iambics to paper. For as it has hap-

pened, the five lines just quoted are the only surviving poetry Byrd ever wrote.

September found him still in London, nigh desperate for amusement. 'Diversions run as low in this town,' he complains to Facetia, 'as good wine in the taverns or charity in the high church; and there would be no comfort at all but for the monsters that come to see and be seen at Bartholomew Fair.' [8]

But these sights were strange, indeed! Cocks with three legs vied for attention with women of three breasts and with a male child of thirty weeks (brachycephalic, probably) whose head, thirty-six inches in circumference, was shown to an astounded populace 'by Her Majesty's expressed order.' [9]

The Queen's interest in this latter case was not abnormal. Her eldest son, the Duke of Buckingham, was then a child of some two years, toddling innocently about the palace, a hopeless victim of the same disease. He died at the age of ten.

The fair itself had long been a British institution. In 1135, Henry I granted a charter to hold it to a courtier who had become Abbot of Saint Bartholomew's, Smithfield. Staged in London, it soon became the greatest attraction of the kingdom, yearly drawing a vast concourse of busy and idle people: gypsies, traffickers, vagabonds, aldermen, and cutpurses from every shire in England. [10] Comic actors of the more boisterous type set up booths there in hopes of supplementing their meager earnings between seasons. Among other prodigies to be seen in 1703, Byrd writes:

There is a horse so surprisingly little that I wonder some lady don't purchase it for her lap. 'Twould be a fit bedfellow for Hideosinda, who for the last century has had none but what she has been forced to buy. Then, Madam, there's an ox of nineteen hands high which, if it had not sustained some disagreeable losses, might be a match for Lacabunda. But there has been got together such a frightful collection of nymphs for actresses that one would swear, as the Plain Dealer has it, that they're all citizen's daughters, lawfully begotten.

The dear ladies that carry the three-fold visor upon their faces of brass, paint, and velvet, flock in coveys to the booths and make a shift to go off there with the toys that are too bad to find a market anywhere else. Now and then comes a fine lady and glitters behind a counter like one of the baubles to be sold, and is both as slight and as dear.[11]

But Facetia's indifference vexed him sorely.

Is there nothing in nature, Madam, can prevail upon you to break this cruel silence [he upbraids her]. The polite diversions of Bartholomew Fair and the pickpockets and visor masks are retired to their starving quarters. Some ladies have had a blessed carnival of it, receiving the pleasure of being picked up under their very husband's horns.... Lord Wharton has had a battle at the Bath with a son of Sir Robert Dashwood, about Mrs. Tempest. The young gentleman went to my lord and charged him with having told about that he had a design to debauch this lady. My Lord replied he never said so and whoever believed it was a fool. The young man went away appearing well satisfied with that answer; but upon digesting the matter he fancied my lordship meant him by what he said, and very foolishly sent him a challenge. They fought a few passes and were separated.[12]

With autumn, Byrd gave up trying. 'The bad weather has come before the courtiers and soldiers,' he wrote her. But these gallants followed soon after. London again became the gay place that he loved. And with theaters opening and friends returning, Facetia was forgotten, doubtless without much effort or remorse.

2

There were few attachments that young Byrd ever formed with the sincerity that characterized his interest in the drama. Nearly one sixth of the 3675 volumes in his library — by long odds the largest ever collected in the colonies [13] — was given over to the works of his contemporaries, the Elizabethans, and to Continental playwrights, both ancient and modern. One can be positive also that he knew at least a few of these authors personally. With Wycherley, he was on terms of extreme intimacy.[14] Rowe and Congreve were among the second- and third-year law students he met when he entered the Temple, and Southerne had finished his training there less than a decade before.

The theater itself, by the time of Anne's ascension in 1702, was considerably rejuvenated. To the Society for the Reformation of Manners, founded in 1690 'for the suppressing of profaneness and debauchery,' [15] nothing appeared so stubborn an obstacle to morality as the many obscenities that had characterized Restoration drama. Among the one hundred thousand persons prosecuted during the half-century of its edifying existence, actors made up an imposing number. King William himself was soon won over to the side of reform. In June, 1697, he issued a warning to all players that he would no longer tolerate their histrionic indecencies, and upon learning in what slight regard his mandate was being held, he caused the following notice to be printed in the London *Gazette*: [16]

His Majesty being informed that notwithstanding his order of June 4, 1697, to prevent profaneness and immorality on the stage, several plays had lately been acted and that actors neglect to leave out such profane and indecent expressions, this is to give notice that those guilty of future violations shall answer for them at their utmost peril.

The survivals of Puritanism were likewise at work. In 1697, Bishop Jeremy Collier published his *Short View of the Immorality and Profaneness of the English Stage.*[17] He was a man of sincere piety, but his attack was cumbrous. In his judgment the drama ought not to be reformed, but abolished. There were replies to the Bishop exposing the weakness in his position. Yet no less a poet than Dryden admitted its essential truth and in his 'Preface to the Fables' repented, realizing that in pandering to the taste of the times he had been false to the cause of true art.[18]

Then there were Steele and Addison, who attacked such vices as gambling and dueling and at the same time praised the superior morality of Shakespeare. When the *Spectator*, therefore, adopted as its aim 'the establishment of a rational standard of conduct in morals, manners, and literature,'[19] the drama of Queen Anne's reign appeared once more well on its way to respectability. But one could never find more than three playhouses open at a time, and Drury Lane and the Queen's Theater, Haymarket, were the only two that could be called financially successful.[20]

Byrd spent many a lively hour at these places. In winter he had to get there at five. By that time it was dark, and with the performance lasting four hours or more, it was always best to begin early. Gallants and ladies would be filing in boisterously to their benches in the pit-like amphitheater. It was the ideal place for young men of quality to see and to be seen. From there one could greet friends of more exclusive tastes whose seats lined the wall beneath the first gallery. In this gallery itself, of course, one found the hoi polloi, whom nobody noticed. The second was occupied by footmen of unusually rough behavior whose masters were supposedly in the pit below.[21]

By no means all the comedy to be witnessed took place upon the stage. On the benches one found, in addition to the young blades already noticed, 'some ladies of reputation and virtue, and abundance of damsels that hunt for prey, who all sit together higgledy piggledy, chatter, toy, play, hear, hear not.' [22] Yet frequently even this normally self-centered group was forced to pause and admire such a remarkable exhibition of talents as Steele describes in one of his Spectator papers. [23]

A very lusty fellow [he recounts], but withal a sort of Beau, got into one of the side boxes before the curtain drew and was disposed to show the whole audience his activity by leaping over the spikes. He passed from this to one of the entering doors where he took snuff with a tolerable good grace, displaying his fine clothes, made two or three feint passes at the curtain with his cane, then faced about and appeared at the other door. Here he affected to survey the whole house, bowed and smiled at random and then showed his teeth, which were some of them indeed very white. After this he retired behind the curtain and obliged us with several views of his person from every opening.

Naturally one was apt to require refreshments during the course of a four to five hour performance. 'Orange wenches' met this emergency by passing about the theater during and between acts, selling fruits ostensibly, and making after-the-show appointments, also ostensibly, with certain of their more interesting customers.

These intermissions were busy occasions, Steele further

informs — especially for the 'rakey young fellows' who had taken the more expensive boxes.

To avoid the clinking dun of a box keeper, at the end of one act they sneak to the opposite side 'till the end of another; then call the box keeper saucy rascal, ridicule the poet, and laugh at the actors.

The women of the town take their places in the pit with their wonted assurance. The middle gallery is filled with the middle part of the city. And your high exalted galleries are graced with handsome footmen who wear their master's linen.[24]

Byrd rarely allowed such incidental fopperies as the one Steele describes to divert his interest seriously from the plays or the actors themselves. This fact is quite evident from one of his letters to Facetia.

The public has lately sustained a very great loss. I don't mean any of our generals either by land or sea — God knows they keep themselves out of harm's way — nor of our Ministers of State who don't fatigue themselves enough to shorten their days. Nor do I mean any prodigious beau or beauty, whose merit, commonly dying before their persons, makes them never missed; but a greater loss than any of these and harder to be supplied. The incomparable Mrs. Verbruggen is dead.

She had more of nature in her acting than any player I did ever see, and was mistress of so easy, so unaffected a manner that nothing but the stage could make me distinguish between the reality and the representation. She had a readiness that never failed an audience. By her death we are robbed of a very great pleasure (which is the dearest thing we could lose), and I think we ought rather to go into mourning for her than for any foreign prince, whose death in all likelihood may be a benefit to the world.[25]

Yet even Byrd's interest in plays must have suffered a temporary waning before the really astounding musical event of January 16, 1705! For on that night no less a phenomenon than grand opera — done in the approved Italian manner, though translated into English — graced the stage of the theater royal at Drury Lane. Of course it is true that the great Purcell's *Dido and Æneas*, 'the first grand opera ever written in conjunction with an original English poem,' [26] had appeared in 1675. But the real Italian flavor was to be found in this present showing of *Arsinoe*,[27] and London society (seemingly inaugurating a virile tradition) made a vast stir about it. Addison was the only one we know whose boorish tastes induced him some years later to voice a slight disappointment in the performance.

The translators of *Arsinoe*, he pointed out, concerned themselves only with making the number of poetic feet in the new English line correspond exactly to those of the Italian. What could be simpler, they reasoned. The words could thus be sung off exactly as scored to the entire satisfaction of the most British of audiences, and even Byrd's 'oyster nymphs' in Billingsgate could follow the action as well as anyone. The only oversight chargeable to these musical Jesuits was that, as a result of their perfect metrics, the finest notes of an air often fell upon the most insignificant words in a sentence. 'I have known the word *and*,' says Addison, 'pursued through the whole gamut; have been entertained with many a melodious *the*; and have heard the most beautiful graces, quavers, and divisions bestowed upon *then*, *for*, and *from*, to the eternal honor of our English particles.' [28]

3

Yet, with all his zest for this brilliant life about him, Byrd's first thirty years were not lacking in personal conditions he might have wished different. Part of the price he paid for an English education was a loss of all real intimacy with his parents. To an extent it was inevitable. At the age of seven he had been sent abroad. He saw his father probably for two or three weeks when that gentleman came over in 1687 to petition the Crown for the office of Receiver-General. In 1698 he returned to Virginia for half a year. This was the only time, except as a child, that he ever saw his mother, for she died in 1699.

Byrd never mentioned her in his writings, doubtless for the reason that he remembered her only indistinctly. But to his father she had been a brave wife. Her high-strung Cavalier spirit had never failed either of them, in all the difficulties of frontier life at the falls. There she had borne his children — one while he was away in New York on a political mission [29] — and lived resolutely alone while three of them were, for their own good, sent to England that they might learn to be gentleman and ladies.

As the elder Byrd grew older, therefore, his life became one of increasing loneliness. In October, 1698, his daughter Ursula Beverley had died, a mother at less than seventeen. Another, Susan, married in London and settled there. Warham, a younger son, had died long before in childhood. One other daughter, Mary, was living in 1700 when he made his will, but nothing further is known of her.[30]

The old gentleman died of the gout in December, 1704.

At that time he was attended only by a housekeeper, Mrs. Jarrett, his man Marant, and by Colonel Randolph, a neighbor who had been sent for earlier in the evening.[31] He had attempted to get up, that he might sign a codicil leaving an annuity of ten pounds to this solitary widow who had looked after him in his last illness.

It was within a few weeks after the *Arsinoe* première that William Byrd II received news of his father's death. He sailed at once for the colony, arriving there in the spring of 1705. By the terms of the will the entire fortune, except for a few minor bequests, was left to him.[32] In land it amounted to approximately twenty-six thousand acres.

It must have been with some strangeness, upon his return, that Byrd looked down upon the graves of the mother and father he remembered so vaguely amid numberless other, old-world memories. Somehow these two had long ceased to be real to him, except the father, possibly, when he had needed help. They had been able to renounce England completely, its gay friendships and its culture as well. The son had already found the task harder — perhaps lacked the strength to renounce it at all. At every opportunity he went back, returning only when threatened with ruin. And when, finally, age and accumulating debts had settled him for a certainty in Virginia, and most of his English friends were dead or had forgotten him, he lived his old life over and over, in the many pictures suspended from his walls, and in the books he had read for the first time in London.

IV

ESQUIRE OF PARTS

About the middle of the year, 'not only with her father's consent but at his earnest desire' (as Byrd afterwards expressed it), he married Lucy, the younger of the two legitimate daughters of Colonel Daniel Parke.

I

DURING the course of his seventy years William Byrd rubbed shoulders with life in more ways, perhaps, than any other Virginian one knows of who died before the Revolution. He was everything except soldier and preacher, and why he has few claims to distinction in these two professions it is not difficult to see. England's break with France, as it actively affected the colonial military situation, did not occur until some ten years after his death. Prior to that time, except for occasional frontier Indian disturbances, the colony was at peace. The ministry was out of the question chiefly because a relatively wealthy parentage and a wholesome love of living had combined to exclude him definitely from it in the interest of something far more attractive.

Yet neither of these callings can justly be regarded as foreign to him. He was constantly alive to the military needs of the colonies, avid, when Councillor, as shall be seen, in urging Spanish expulsion from Carthagena, and highly apprehensive of French encroachments west of the Alleghanies.[1] His advice was always on the side of intelligent foresight in the way of preparedness, or a quick decisive movement that would crush an enemy as well as surprise him. Half measures he invariably regarded with contempt.

In his library, on the other hand, the works on divinity alone numbered three hundred volumes.[2] All the Church Fathers were represented. He had his Scriptures in Dutch, Hebrew, Greek, or Latin, and Ricaud's *Lives of the Popes* beside the sermons of Tillotson and Bishop Hall. And for the last sixteen years of his life he was a constant friend and patron of the Reverend Peter Fontaine, his parish minister. He took him along to convert the North Carolinians when the dividing line was run in 1728 and selected him a few months before his death as one of the three witnesses to his will.

Yet Byrd was much more. In addition to being Councillor, judge, lawyer of really exceptional ability, planter constantly experimenting with new seeds or growths, and merchant, he was an author when few Virginians knew what it was to write anything except propaganda. And he wrote — though the twentieth-century mind finds it difficult to understand — not for publication primarily, but for the quiet diversion of those few friends in England with whom he had been most intimate. His works were printed for the first time in 1841, ninety-seven years after his death.[3]

His interest in the drama has been already noticed. Painting was also a source of real enjoyment to him. As a young man he sat for Kneller, the most famous artist of the first part of his century, who, as Ashton phrases it, 'had been knighted by William, petted by Anne, and baroneted by George I.'[4] Years later he patronized the portrait painter, Charles Bridges, who had had the temerity to come to Virginia in search of a livelihood. Byrd had Bridges do his children and then sent him on to former Governor Spotswood with a highly favorable recommendation to the effect that, 'had he lived so long ago as when places were given to the most deserving, he might have pretended to be sergeant painter of Virginia.' [5]

Finally, in what may be reckoned a very real sense, William Byrd was a man of science, thus again placing himself in curious intellectual isolation from the mass of his fellow Virginians. His talent consisted in an ability to carry on constant investigations of a botanical or medicinal nature without permitting the restrictiveness of such subjects to dwarf him as a social personality. Primarily, and always, in its broadest implications, he was concerned with living the life of a cultivated gentleman.

But it must be said that in the field of medicine strange notions were abroad. And Byrd, like Drs. Sloane and Garth, two leading London contemporaries and friends, doubtless shared them dogmatically. Blood-letting and purging, for example, were regarded as without doubt the principal remedies for any disease. It was likewise such notables as these who many times approved of live toads in cases of dropsy or smallpox, who prescribed white dung of a peacock, when dried, with considerable confidence to yellow jaundice sufferers, and who recommended live hog lice, new gathered earthworms, inward skins of capons' gizzards, or goose dung gathered in the springtime [6] with quite as much confidence and occasionally as good results as medicines are given today.

With early eighteenth-century science thus in what may at best be called an elementary stage, and with medicine, among other of its branches, destined for a complete transformation with the advent of antiseptic surgery, the germ theory of disease, and anæsthesia, it does not appear unfair to estimate a man of that day by his interest in the subject as well as by what results he achieved. So considered, Byrd's position is one of importance.

His election to membership in the Royal Society he doubtless owed to Sir Robert Southwell, who was president of that body from 1690 to 1695, and who until his death seven years later never ceased to be greatly enthusiastic about its work. As far as their published 'Transactions' are indicative, Byrd's connection with this group led to very little. He is represented by only one paper, communicated in 1697 and called 'An account of a Negro Boy that is Dappled in several places of his Body with White Spots.' [7] But his letters to Sir Hans Sloane, secretary of the Society from 1692 to 1712 and president, after Sir Isaac Newton, from 1727 to his death in 1741, show that he investigated a great deal, even if after his twenty-third year nothing was formally presented. This correspondence began soon after Byrd's return to the colony.

The news of my father's death hurried me so suddenly from England [he writes in April, 1706],[8] that I had not time to receive the commands either of the society or of yourself; and the infinite deal of business I have had since my arrival has not permitted me to furnish myself with any observations upon the country. This may be allowed to be a very reasonable excuse for me, who found all my private affairs in great disorder after having been eight months without an owner. And besides that, my lord treasurer has laid his commands upon me to pass all my father's public accounts over again, which are of seventeen years standing; and I have been wholly employed upon that, to the neglect of my own necessary business, that I might be in condition to obey his lordship's commands before the sailing of the fleet.

He goes on to lament the absence of scientists in a country where there is such a variety of natural specimens unobserved. 'Here be some men indeed that are called doctors, but they are generally discarded surgeons of ships who know nothing above the very common remedies.' 'Ignorant newspapers which play it up that the country is very unhealthy' also come in for their share of condemnation. Most cases of agues, a common distemper they write about, are due in his opinion to the intemperance with which people in Virginia eat fruit. Their only measure, he declares, is 'the bigness of their bellies.'

Byrd adds that he has set his countrymen a stirring example against such complaints and against taking colds by adjusting his body to abrupt changes in temperature. For the whole of the previous winter he went for a plunge in the river twice each week 'without once being discouraged by frost or snow.' At first, he admits, he was taken for a madman, but by spring his neighbors appeared reconciled to the practice, though none had offered to join him.

He sent a small box of rattlesnake root with his letter. It was a remedy employed constantly by the Indians and by English traders in curing themselves and their horses of such bites, and had been used by his own servants with uniform success. This box also contained a sample of true 'hypoquecuana' and another root that had been strongly recommended for 'dry gripes and wind colic.' Byrd wanted expert opinion on both specimens.

When I have more time [he concluded], I hope to be able to do more service. In the meantime do me the justice to believe that nobody has better inclinations to promote natural knowledge than myself, and if you will direct me after what manner I may be most serviceable to the society and to the commonwealth of learning, I will readily obey you. If you have anything curious there I should be obliged to you if you'll please to favor me with a knowledge of it. [9]

Byrd's letter of September 10, 1708, is equally informing. Since writing he had tried without success to grow 'hippecoacanna' in his own garden. He sends along some poke berries which he thinks good dye material 'if we understood the right way of preparing it. For the good of my country, therefore, I beg of you to tell me the best ways to fix dyes, of which we are very ignorant.' [10]

This shipment also included samples of the Jamestown weed, believed to be very poisonous, and the seed of the Jerusalem oak, 'which kills worms better than any worm seed I ever heard of.' He added his personal testimony in behalf of rattlesnake root as a cure for diarrhœa when taken in a little canary, tonic fashion. Incidentally, truth forced him to confess that he contracted this last-named illness through his wintery plunges in the James, and that he had deemed it wise to discontinue them.

Byrd wrote again in June, 1710, explaining the difficulty he had encountered in shipping Sloane thirty pounds of 'hippecoacanna' [11] the year before. It had been taxed at the customs house at the rate of forty shillings a pound, and was hard to get in the first place. He said he would go to some trouble to procure a greater supply, provided the secretary would make it worth while. 'If it be necessary to pay customs, I must submit, but do hope you'll have interest enough to get it custom free.'

Byrd had become attracted by the possibilities of profit in this medicine and offered Sloane the customary broker's fee of two and one half per cent, if he could manage to dispose of it in London. 'I wish you'd please to let me know how the Royal Society thrives,' he adds, 'and to assure 'em that I shall always be ready to do 'em what service I can in this country. I further beg of you to send me your account of Jamaica, and if there be any other good voyage published since I left England, or any other curious piece, to send it to me and pay yourself out of the profits of the cargo.' [12]

Meanwhile our country gentleman was meeting with mingled success and failure in other quarters. Shortly after the elder Byrd's death, one Blackiston, a London attorney, was complaisant enough to petition the Lords of Trade that Byrd be awarded his father's seat in the Council.[13] This body replied by stating that, though it entertained a very high opinion of Mr. Byrd's ability, Messrs. John Smith and John Lewis had previously been recommended for the honor and that their claims were the more deserving.

He was more fortunate regarding the auditorship. By an order of the Queen, dated April 2, 1705,[14] he was confirmed as his father's successor, though at that time he had not yet reached Virginia. But the office was soon robbed of half its importance. For some years past, Byrd explains, two men in particular, 'I. B. and B. H., did several times endeavor to get the place divided, upon pretence of the incompatibility of the auditor and receiver being one person.' [15]

At first, these reformers met with little success. The Council was quite content with its traditional practice of having both offices in the hands of one of its trusted members, requiring him merely to submit his reports to a cursory examination by a Councillor committee before sending them on to England. But after a while the agitators for a more efficient system took the matter before the Lords of Trade, who asked the Council for a written opinion. In defense of its established policy, this body contended that the salary attached to the place was too small to be of advantage to more than one man, and urged that no changes be made. This reason was sound enough. The complete audit Byrd made of his father's accounts, which was accepted in England without cavil, showed that the highest yearly income he ever received from the position amounted to only one hundred and thirty pounds. On many occasions it fell considerably below this figure.[16] It is safe to say that for the seventeen years he averaged not more than one hundred pounds, though the law allowed him seven and one half per cent of all collections.

But before these convincing statistics reached them, the Lords of Trade concluded that all temptation to defraud Her Majesty could be obviated by commissioning a second party as auditor of the Receiver-General's books. The honor fell to Dudley Digges, who was appointed October 10, 1705. Seven days later, Byrd was re-declared Receiver-General at a salary of three per cent. It required a decade of desultory complaining to raise this fraction to five.

2

Yet Byrd was living but half a life! Here it was 1706. He had passed his thirty-second year, was the owner of more than twenty-five thousand acres, Receiver-General of Her Majesty's revenue in Virginia, highly sociable, fond especially of fine ladies — but unmarried. He began looking about with some concern for a means of remedying this unnatural state, and before long things had, easily enough, been put aright. About the middle of the year, 'not only with her father's consent, but at his earnest desire' [17] (as Byrd afterwards expressed it), he married Lucy, the younger of the two legitimate daughters of Colonel Daniel Parke.

The head of this family was somewhat notorious. It was a matter of common gossip, for example, that the interesting young lady he had brought over to Virginia in 1696, and to whom he referred with a certain suspicious vagueness as his cousin, was no relative at all, but a shameless mistress. Commissary Blair, among others who preached to the aristocracy of Bruton Church, Williamsburg, was in no frame of mind to permit so vicious a flouting of the Seventh Commandment to go unchallenged. He held forth Sunday after Sunday upon an extraordinarily withering area in hell reserved solely for the adulterer. Impudently handsome gallant though he was, Parke could not but feel a certain uneasiness with the uncomfortable expatiations of this man of God in his ears. It seemed — a weltering sensation in itself — as though everyone were staring fixedly at the back of his neck; and with this red-faced Scotchman glaring his holy wrath upon him from an exalted place in the pulpit, things were fast becoming entirely too personal. Within a very few weeks Daniel Parke decided that life was vastly more tolerable without these weekly messages from such a menacing spokesman of the Holy Spirit, and discontinued his church attendance entirely. But he was biding his time.

It came during Andros's break with the Commissary, while Byrd was representing the former at the Lambeth Conference. At the Governor's instigation, it is said, Parke was induced to return to the services one Sunday. Now Mrs. Blair, the Commissary's wife, had no pew of her own. For some time she had made a habit of accepting an invitation to occupy that one reserved for Lady Berkeley's husband, who was Parke's father-in-law by an earlier marriage. On this particular occasion Parke strutted in as usual, and when he noticed Mrs. Blair in this pew, he 'pretended to regard it as his own, and rushing up with a mighty violence, seized her by the wrist and pulled her out in the presence of the minister and congregation, who were greatly scandalized, as they ought to have been, by this ruffianly and profane action.' [18]

For this truly unchivalrous deed Parke found himself all but ostracized from Virginia society, and, with Andros's recall, deemed it wise to return to London. His handsome face soon recommended him to the Marlboroughs, and he was made an aide to the Duke in his campaign in the Low Countries. The favor was given him, after the battle of Blenheim, of carrying the tidings of this glorious victory to the Queen. Her Majesty was highly impressed with his appearance and rewarded him with a medallion containing her likeness — which he wore constantly thereafter upon his breast — and with the governorship of the Leeward

Islands.[19] Thus, when Byrd began his attentions to Lucy Parke, the favor of a queen had considerably atoned for the earlier ungallantries of her father.

There is only one thing regarding this marriage itself about which one can feel certain: it was entirely conventional and orthodox. It is impossible to imagine William Byrd doing anything not sanctioned by the best social usage. Doubtless he followed the tradition of colonial times by securing the approval of Parke before he began any serious advances toward his daughter's hand,[20] obtained at least a tacit understanding about the settlement intended for her, and found the young lady well-informed through her parent of his own highly inviting prospects. It was never very wise entirely to lose one's head in such a matter, for there were economic complications that could easily be jeopardized if one were bent merely upon following one's heart. Imagine, for example, getting one's self in John Rolfe's emotional predicament — becoming so enamoured of the Indian Pocahontas that he wrote another man (the Governor at that) such an intrinsically foolish confession as 'my heart and best thoughts are and have been a long tyme soe intangled and enthralled in soe intricate a laborinth that I am even awearied to unwynde myselfe thereout!' [21] To a student of Descartes and Locke, it was absurd.

Byrd's disposition was extremely agreeable. It would be a simple matter for him to live pleasantly with any lady whose temper was not positively shrewish. He looked upon the romantic effusions and dallying with which women of his own and subsequent generations have been wooed as rather silly adjuncts to an otherwise sensible business, demanded by custom and therefore to be complied with gracefully. After marriage things were of course rationalized, though 'some fond females,' he observed once with evident disgust, 'fancy people should love with as little reason after marriage as before.' [22] This, in his opinion, was carrying the jest entirely too far.

He believed quite as heartily in marrying within one's social circle. If a person were a freeholder, he should by all means wed into such a family. If an indentured servant, he should remain in that caste. Such a view seems extraordinary when one considers how rapidly Byrd and his father had themselves transcended the position of even a seventeenth-century London tradesman. But this phenomenon they doubtless attributed to a change from an old to a new world environment and to naturally superior native endowments.

When Byrd visited Spotswood's mines in 1732, he expressed himself quite forcibly on the subject. The intervals of such a ten-day journey were, of course, spent at the homes of the more prosperous planters along the way. While being entertained by one Mrs. Fleming, he writes, 'I learned all the tragical story of her daughter's humble marriage with her uncle's overseer.' As overseers were nearly always former indentured servants, such a union involved a distinct loss of caste.

Besides the meanness of this mortal's aspect [he continues], the man has not one visible qualification, except impudence, to recommend him to a female's inclinations. But there is sometimes such a charm in that Hibernian endowment that frail woman can't withstand it, though it stand alone without any other recommendation. Had she run away with a gentleman or a

pretty fellow, there might have been some excuse for her, though
he were of inferior fortune. But to stoop to a dirty plebeian,
without any kind of merit, is the lowest prostitution. I found
the family justly enraged at it, and though I had more good
nature than to join in her condemnation, yet I could devise no
excuse for so senseless a prank as this young gentlewoman had
played.[23]

3

Byrd's appointment to the Council came August 18,
1708. Acting upon the recommendation of the absentee
Governor Hunter and of Micajah Perry — that same
prominent London merchant who had had business dealings with his father and whose importunities for unpaid
debts were to harass him so sorely as he grew older — the
Queen on that date ordered that he was to be 'of the Council of Virginia in the place of John Lightfoot, deceased.'[24]
September 12 of the following year he took the prescribed
oaths of secrecy and of obedience to the Crown and was
duly admitted to membership. The day was a memorable
one. It marked his permanent elevation to what was, indeed, the acme of social, political, and economic prominence. From that date Byrd was a Virginia aristocrat in
the most exclusive sense of the term — a sense that for the
colonies, as for the subsequent states, was truly unique.

This body consisted of twelve members, appointed for
life who, with the Governor or Lieutenant-Governor as its
president, composed the upper house of the Assembly. It
was expressly declared in the instructions received by the
Governor from time to time that no one was to be chosen
Councillor known to be lacking in estate or in ability.[25]

When the Governor was away, or during the intervals between the death of one and the arrival of a successor, the
oldest Councillor in service acted in his stead. In association with the Governor these men likewise formed the
General Court, which concentrated in itself the several
jurisdictions of the chancery, king's bench, common pleas,
exchequer, admiralty, and ecclesiastical courts of England.[26] From a military standpoint, they served as com-
manders-in-chief or colonels of their respective groups of
counties, and as such possessed privileges closely analogous
to those of the English Lord's Lieutenants.

It is not going too far [one is told] to say that Council members
appropriated to themselves all the higher offices of the colony
which were attended with the largest salaries or presented the
most numerous chances for money getting. They deliberately
disregarded the fact that the concentration of these offices in so
few hands brought about serious damage to the public interests
whenever the councillor assumed the duties of two separate
positions really in conflict with each other. A councillor, for
instance, was called on to pass upon the correctness of his own
accounts as collector [as was Byrd's father]. As collector he was
obliged, for his own enlightenment as a judge of the general
court, to inform himself of all violations of the Navigation Acts.
As a farmer of quit-rents he practically owed the success of his
bid to himself as councillor. As escheator, who was a ministerial
officer, he took and returned the inquisitions of escheats to himself as a judicial officer, and as such passed upon the points of
law coming up in his own inquisitions.[27]

Serving as Councillor under these circumstances should
have been sufficient to appease any reasonable public am-
bitions one might have entertained. But this was rarely
the case. It has well been said that 'no office, provided

it carried a salary, was too insignificant to be coveted by the most conspicuous or even by the wealthiest citizens. Coroner, appraiser of property, viewer, escheator, member of the vestry, sheriff, clerk — all could claim that from the number as well as from the importance of their official positions they were the very first men in their community.' [28]

One of the least salutary of the effects produced by this concentration of power was that at times the affairs of an entire district, or of the colony even, would be in the hands of a single family. Between 1670 and 1691, for instance, every political office in Henrico County, Byrd's birthplace, was occupied either by a Randolph, a Cocke, or a Ferrar. During the greater part of this interval, the clerkship of the county court was filled by William or Henry Randolph, and the court which convened in April, 1698, included at least three members of the Cocke family, while a fourth served as clerk. By 1703 the situation had reached such a stage that the Burwells, through themselves and their blood relations, controlled the decisions of the Council itself and, in consequence, of the General Court. Spotswood bitterly complained that should a cause involving a Burwell come to trial, seven of its twelve members, owing to their kinship to that family, would have to retire from the deliberation of the case.[29]

Byrd was in England when this startling assertion became known, and the Lords of Trade asked him for the facts. In November, 1717, he appeared before them, practically confirming the charge, though at the time he was decidedly at odds with the Governor. Of the entire membership, he stated, six of them — Edmund Jenings, Robert Carter, John Smith, John Lewis, William Cocke, and Mann Page — 'were not related to any of the Council.' But he was compelled to admit that James Blair and Philip Ludwell had both married sisters of a fellow Councillor, Nathaniel Harrison, that he had himself married Ludwell's niece, that William Bassett and Edmund Berkeley had married half-nieces of Ludwell, and that Harrison's sister was Ludwell's wife.[30]

Naturally such a collocation of power was jealously guarded by these gentlemen. They passed laws especially designed to augment it. In 1678 they asserted that during their term of office they were exempt from arrest by all usual processes of law. Hartwell declared twenty years later that he knew of no means by which a member of the Council could be brought into court to answer to the most ordinary case brought against him there.[31] To slander one of them was considered as great a crime as defaming the Governor's own person. The martial code provided three successive whippings for the first offense, three years' hard labor in the galleys for the second, and death for the third.[32]

Complaints against this group of dignitaries were, naturally, by no means infrequent. Bacon had singled them out, though at a time when through Berkeley's senile favoritism conditions were worse than usual, as 'wicked and pernicious aiders and assistors against the commonalty.' [33] The Lords of Trade tried bravely to curtail the autocratic tendencies Bacon complained of. In 1680 they demanded of the Council a quarterly journal comprising accounts 'of all matters, civil, ecclesiastical, and military, councillor debates and results on the framing of laws.' [34] This order was made more inclusive by two separate commands of King

Charles, issued within the following eighteen months.[35] But if designed as anything beyond a formality, His Majesty's decrees were without effect. Nearly two decades later, Benjamin Harrison wrote the Lords of Trade that 'the Councillors would always have so great a regard to their own interests that they would not fail to stand by each other in opposition to all persons whatsoever.' [36]

Like politicians the world over, these gentlemen made the most of what opportunities for fraud their positions afforded by acquiring unfairly tracts of land ranging anywhere from twenty thousand to two hundred thousand acres. By way of justifying themselves, they doubtless reasoned that, with a yearly salary of but three hundred and fifty pounds divided among the twelve of them,[37] any aberrations from the letter of the law were amply warranted. After all, did not one owe some things to one's family?

The three conditions under which land rightfully could be had were simple enough. One acquired it 'by taking a patent upon a survey of new land, by petition for land lapsed, or by petition for land escheated. The conditions of the two former are an entry of rights; the condition of the third a composition of two pounds of tobacco for every acre.' [38] Anyone who moved to Virginia was entitled by the royal charter to a grant of fifty acres for himself and to another fifty for each additional member of his family, or for immigrants who had been induced to follow him. To hold this land it was necessary to build a house of some sort, to pay an annual quit-rent fee or tax at the rate of two shillings for every one hundred acres, and to plant at least three out of each fifty acres granted.[39] For the average farmer of honest intentions, this was not a bad arrangement at all. But when a man found himself taxed for one hundred thousand acres or more, even two shillings a hundred often amounted to sums that he found it distressing to pay.

In truth, it is not strange to be told that

the wealthy planters consistently avoided the payment of these taxes. Their enormous power in the colonial government made this an easy matter, for the collectors and sheriffs in the various counties found it convenient not to question their statements of the extent of their property, while no one dared prosecute them even when glaring cases of fraud came to light. Estates of fifty or sixty thousand acres often yielded less in quit-rents than plantations of one third their size. Sometimes the planters refused to pay taxes at all on their land and no penalty was inflicted on them. Chilton, in 1697, declared that the Virginians would be forced to resign their patents to huge tracts of country if the government should demand the arrears of quit-rents.

Even greater frauds were perpetrated by prominent men [this writer continues] in securing patents for land. The laws requiring that the public territory should be granted only in small parcels, that a house should be built upon each, and that a part should be put under cultivation were continually neglected. If they wished to keep within the limits of the law, they constructed but slight shanties, so small and ill-made that no human being could inhabit them. On one grant of 27,107 acres the house cost less than ten shillings. In another case a sheriff found in a single county 30,000 acres upon which nothing existed that could be distrained for quit-rents.[40]

Amid numerous acts of deception and fraud, several are conspicuous. Colonel Philip Ludwell had brought forty immigrants into the colony. According to the law in force since the days of the London Company, this entitled him to a grant of two thousand acres of land. After securing the patent, he changed the record with his own hand by adding one cipher each to the forty and two thousand, making the figures four hundred and twenty thousand respectively. In this way he obtained ten times the property due him, and despite the fraud being notorious at the time, so great was his influence that his rights went unquestioned.[41]

Alexander Spotswood, just before his retirement, was guilty of a theft even greater than Ludwell's. His successor, Drysdale, wrote the Lords of Trade in 1724 that he 'finds Colonel Spotswood had a great regard for his own private interest. Two tracts of land, one of twenty thousand and another of forty thousand acres, being patented under borrowed names for his use, have since been conveyed to him, for which he has neither paid rights nor given either sort of bond to pay if demanded or to surrender.' [42] The temptation had apparently proved too much even for a governor to resist.

And there is little evidence to show that conditions improved as Byrd grew older. During the last fifteen years of his life, the Scotch-Irish began their migrations into the Shenandoah Valley. And Governor Gooch, it is said, was then dispensing the lands there so freely that one Jacob Stoner — not a councillor at all — secured many acres by giving his cattle human names as settlers, 'and a young woman, by dressing in various disguises of masculine attire, obtained several large farms.' [43] The members of a rapidly growing middle class were apparently not backward in adopting methods so long established by their more powerful brothers.

Yet this vast power did not acquire its feudal proportions

without surviving successfully at least one vigorous challenge. A few months after Byrd assumed his seat there arrived in Virginia as Governor, Alexander Spotswood — a man who fought the Councillors' usurpation of authority with a clear-headed foresight and fairness that no colonial Virginia Governor ever before or afterwards approached. But even Spotswood wavered at length. The struggle had begun to grow futile, and the odds were too great. Besides, it was hardly worth while to contend always against one's fellows when an honorable truce was possible, and with it more wealth than could be hoped for while serving strictly as a king's representative. But it required ten years to break this courageous Scotchman's spirit — and those years were indeed unpleasant ones, for William Byrd of Westover in particular.

V

HASTY BARGAINER

'In short, a man must be either his dog or his ass, neither of which stations suits
in the least with my constitution.'

I

DURING the first four years of Byrd's marriage, his wife
bore him a daughter and a son. Evelyn, as shall be seen,
was destined to be educated in England and, if tradition
may be relied upon, to be courted desperately by one of the
most notorious old rakes of George I's reign. But young
Parke died an infant in 1710.

The same year, the grandfather for whom he was named
met a violent end at Antigua. Since first coming to the
Leeward Islands, this favorite of the Hero of Blenheim
and of Queen Anne — 'ever ready at giving a challenge,
especially before company, like the greatest Hector in
town' [1] — had been unpopular. His high-handed administrative policy at length brought on a riot, in the course
of which he was murdered. The event occurred just at
the time of the Marlborough party's fall, and the succeeding Whig administration did not trouble itself to avenge
him.

Parke's will was peculiar. It was found to have been
made shortly before his death, and by its terms all his
property in Virginia and England was left to his eldest
daughter Frances, who had married John Custis. 'And his
estate in the West Indies (which was of twice the value of
all the rest) went to Lucy Chester, whom he had too much

reason to believe his own daughter, although her mother
was at that time a married woman. As for Mrs. Byrd,' her
irate husband continues, 'who had never offended her
father — she was fobbed off with £1000.' [2] A second
natural offspring, Julius Cæsar Parke, was left an annuity
of fifty pounds for life. It looked as though the gods were
standing up for bastards in earnest.

All the debts and legacies involved were charged against
the Virginia and English properties, and Custis, Micajah
Perry, Thomas Lane, and Richard Perry were named
executors.[3] These encumbrances were considerable. Perry
wrote Byrd about 1712 that Parke owed his firm £2400,
£1500 more to three English women, and that a certain
estate he had had at Whitechurch, Dorset, was worth
£4000, but mortgaged to the extent of £2230.[4] An additional £400 was due the Queen as interest on Parke's
bond.

Now the sum with which his wife had been 'fobbed off'
was hardly as insignificant as Byrd chose to consider it.
One has no reason to suppose that he was not soon paid in
cash; and since money, according to careful estimate,[5]
amounted to fifteen times its present value, one conjectures
that a more circumspect economist would have been reasonably content with the agreement.

Not so with Byrd. As a member of Her Majesty's Council he had already begun to catch the general and highly
popular fever of land acquisition. For little sums he was
buying here and there (though mostly adjoining the holdings left him by his father near the falls of the James) tracts
of from two to four hundred acres. The cost was small. In
1707, William Randolph sold him 223 acres near this place

for seventeen pounds, and a few years later he bought another 408–acre tract in the same county.[6]

In making these investments, Byrd was following the sober convictions of a lifetime. 'I must needs be of your opinion,' he wrote Francis Otway in 1736, 'to convert as much of your income as possible into ground rents, which will withstand every calamity but an earthquake. Houses, God knows, are a very uncertain estate, lying at the mercy of fire and tempest, and though they be so lucky as to escape these disasters, will be subject to decay and consequently to repairs. And this will bring the plague or workmen, who make no bones of abusing the honest landlord as much as they can.'[7]

It must have been due to this thoroughly ingrained though not unimpeachable idea that Byrd made his sad bargain with Parke's executors. The prospect of extensive properties, by right at least partly his wife's, being turned over to the enjoyment of strangers was more than his family pride could endure. In the whole affair he had virtually been ignored, and to a man of his ability this was almost an affront. Accordingly, Byrd thrust himself before the welcome attention of Custis (who for more than a year had been at his wits' end trying to realize some profit from the estate) and in February, 1711, the two reached the following agreement:

That the said John Custis and Frances his wife shall by sufficient conveyance give and grant all the land, houses, mills and slaves to the said William Byrd and his heirs forever which are mentioned in an act of the Assembly entitled 'An act to enable John Custis and Frances his wife to dispose of certain lands etc. belonging to the late Collo. Parke, to pay the debts and legacies of the said Parke.'

That everything continue on the plantations to the use of the said William Byrd that now is upon the same.

That all tobacco sent to England, and all the tobacco already made upon any of the plantations belonging to the late Collo. Daniel Parke and not yet sent to England, be and remain to the use of the said William Byrd.

That all effects of any sort now in England remain to the use of the said Byrd which did belong to the late Collo. Parke and likewise all arrears of rent, all moneys due upon account, and all moneys or effects whatsoever belonging to the late Parke in any way, to belong to the said William Byrd.

In consideration thereof the said William Byrd doth hereby oblige himself, his heirs, executors, and administrators to pay all the debts due in England from the late Collo. Parke and charged upon his estate in Virginia and all the legacies charged upon his Virginia estate by his last will and testament and thereof shall discharge the said John Custis and Frances his wife and their heirs forever.[8]

A memorandum attached to the above contract bore an additional significant clause:

If any debts appear to have been due from the late Collo. Parke in Virginia before the time that John Custis took care of the said estate they shall be equally paid, one moiety by John Custis and the other moiety by William Byrd. But all since by John Custis.[9]

Nothing could have been simpler. Custis, as the agreement itself implies, had already been forced to obtain legislative permission that he might sell part of Parke's Virginia property to pay the legacies then due.[10] Byrd took the whole matter off his hands and left him with a considerably reduced but entirely unencumbered fortune. In England, the Perrys were overjoyed. They had been quite disgusted with the ample provisions their debtor had made for his illegitimate children, and the prospect of a responsible party assuming his obligations appeared as pleasant a thing as could reasonably be imagined. They joined with Byrd, who soon decided to dispose of Parke's mill, by petitioning the Queen for her necessary consent,[11] and the request was soon granted.

Indeed, if such an unworthy suspicion is at all pardonable, one might even hazard saying that the Perrys' enthusiasm so far overmastered their scruples as to induce them to list Parke's indebtedness in England and at what they knew to be considerably below its true figure. Definite proof either way is, perhaps, not to be had. One is told that the schedule already mentioned [12] — amounting to only £6130 — was sent Byrd 'about 1712.' [13] But in all probability he received it the year before and, trusting to its correctness, entered into the above agreement with his brother-in-law. From a second statement,[14] that reached Byrd, more than likely, after he signed with Custis, it appears that the debts in England were given as £8510, or £2380 in excess of the first sum. In 1713, soon after he learned of the disparity in these two accounts, Byrd petitioned the Lords of Trade for permission to visit England upon 'private business.' [15]

There can be little doubt but that the more accurate disclosures of the Perrys had by this time made a personal investigation imperative. The fact one finds difficult to reconcile with the widely known business efficiency of these gentlemen is that apparently, though themselves Parke's English executors and creditors, they had no intelligent idea at all of the extent of his obligations in that country until more than a year after his death and until, incidentally, Byrd had bargained to pay them.

Even under the lesser schedule, Byrd was well aware that the responsibility he had assumed was a grave one. 'Whenever there happens an opportunity of writing to England,' he said to Custis the day they signed their agreement, 'don't fail to entreat Mr. Perry's favor, and let my sister set her shoulders to it, that the burden I have taken upon my back may be as light as possible.' [16] He went over the details of the contract at considerable length in another letter posted three days later. 'I hope your intention was the same with mine in these particulars,' he then concluded, 'so that there may not be the least jarr between us; but to have things plain and clear is necessary on both sides, and I can protest I will pretend to nothing that was not my true meaning at the signing our articles, without any gripeing or surprize.' [17]

But 'gripeing' and regrettable 'surprize' came none the less. In 1723 he wrote Custis, complaining of Perry's charging to his account several things that had turned up since Parke's death.

I herewith send you a copy of them, that you may be convinced they belong not to me to pay, as you will find by reading over the last paragraph of my articles with you. I have let Mr. Perry know I will by no means allow them, but that he must apply himself to those who by the will are obliged to pay the debts, so that I suppose you will soon hear from him on the subject. For my part [he added], I have already paid more by £1000 than appeared in the list of debts which was sent me before I contracted with you, but as I had obliged myself thereto, I submitted. [18]

The worst one can say for Byrd in this unfortunate affair is that he took an unwise chance and, moved by a compelling desire for property, relied too greatly upon certain merchants. But a little sympathy might induce one to add that, considered from a more skeptical angle, he may be regarded quite as reasonably as the innocent victim of a deliberate fraud, perpetrated by two of his supposed English friends.

2

Almost from the beginning of his appointment, Byrd took an active part in the business of the Council. He was on the best of terms with Spotswood; and with Commissary Blair's assistance his colleagues ordered him in December, 1710, to prepare two addresses: the first expressing gratitude to the Crown for favors lately bestowed on the colony, and a second to their own new Lieutenant-Governor recounting 'the happiness of the country under his prudent administration.'[19] The following year this body ordered Byrd and John Lewis to present another statement of confidence to Spotswood. They approved most particularly his 'frugal management and singular diligence in putting the country in a posture of defense.'[20]

This last-named endorsement referred especially to certain North Carolina Indian troubles that were beginning to threaten the peace of Virginia. The Assembly of the former colony was fast proving itself unable to cope with the situation and had already made several appeals to neighboring provinces for help. Some attention to the matter is of importance in affording an understanding of Byrd's own subsequent attitude toward North Carolinians in general.

Members of the Virginia House of Burgesses, representing a more generally public sentiment, had oddly enough favored aiding their sister colony from the start. On November 28, 1711, they urgently requested that the Governor declare war on the Tuscarora Nation 'because of the horrid barbarities, murthers, and hostilities lately committed upon Her Majesty's subjects there.' [21] Spotswood complied only so far as to allow the appointment of rangers. But these men were placed under definite restrictions. They could not kill an Indian unless when challenged he resisted or attempted to flee, and their salary was to be at a rate of five thousand pounds of tobacco a year — the approximate equivalent of twenty-five pounds.

Three months later, finding this provision ineffective, a considerable number of North Carolina citizens themselves petitioned Spotswood that 'whereas there hath, by ye permition of Almighty God for our sins and Desobedance, bin a most horred massecre committed by ye Tuscarora Indens upon Her Majesty's pore subjects... and we who by God's Providence have survived are in continual Dread and do suffer Dayley destruction in our stocks and horses and fenceing being burned — which if not speedaly prevented we must all likewise Perrish, there being no care taken to prevent it in our country...' they therefore 'with one voyse' implore military assistance against 'ye Barbarous Insolency of these Rebelous rogues.' [22]

But Spotswood's hands were now tied by the Council. He wrote Governor Pollock of North Carolina in December, 1712, that he was uncertain how to proceed in the matter, for his upper house had expressed certain scruples against declaring war against the Indians before their neighboring government had itself done so. He had taken most of the one thousand pounds raised by the Virginia Assembly in the emergency, he added, and bought blankets for the soldiers.

Pollock's reply pictured his province as in most desperate circumstances. Supposedly friendly South Carolina Indians were, plainly, 'very unstable.' The Tuscaroras had fortified themselves in strongholds difficult to assail. The Meharrins, another powerful tribe, were becoming 'very insolent.' And finally, through the ignorance and obstinacy of his own Assembly, the attacking force of nine hundred that he had been able to muster was without food and unable to proceed against the enemy. As for the Virginia Council's scruples, he asserted that his own legislature thought it altogether unnecessary to declare war when for the last fifteen months they had been fighting for their lives. 'Indeed,' he added, 'it does seem to me a little preposterous.' But to remove all cause of complaint between the two governments, he promised shortly to have war formally declared.[23]

Spotswood freely admitted that his disgust with the North Carolinians was attributable chiefly to their Assembly. It was chosen, so he wrote the Lords of Trade, by the mob. Its members had 'declared their resolution to raise no tax on the people.' Their election had been made possible through a defect in their constitution 'which allows every man not a servant, who can purchase half an acre of land, an equal vote with gentlemen holding the best estates in the country.'[24]

This Assembly, he went on to say, promised during the course of the trouble to give adequate provisions to any

Virginia troops he might send to their defense. Acting upon this tentative agreement, Spotswood began mustering an army and, as he said later, 'undertook in the depth of winter a journey to South Key,' well over one hundred miles from Williamsburg. He was to meet Pollock there and confirm the matter. But the latter gentleman failed to appear. 'And it was thought fitting to send to meet me then only two persons who had no other powers than to receive the clothing I had brought for their relief and to hear what I had to propose.' [25] About this time he also learned that his government was expected by his neighbors not only to raise but fully to equip and provision the entire body of troops intended for their assistance.

This was the last straw.

I must now plainly tell you [he wrote Pollock] that after having been twice baffled by your Assembly, I am discouraged from undertaking anything further for your relief… for I have not been used to make war after the Indian manner without any measures concerted or promises regarded…. You needed not have given yourself so much trouble to apologize for the delay of your Assembly's address, for it is the mismanagement of weighty affairs and not the miscarriage of such trivial matters that can affect me. [26]

This proved in truth to be the end of the question, until Colonel Moore, unaided by other than his fellow colonists and a few friendly Indians, vanquished the enemy and demolished their fort. Spotswood then did condescend to arrange an honorable peace between the Carolinians and what Tuscaroras remained alive.

As a member of the Virginia Council, Byrd shared in its entirety the contempt Spotswood entertained for the vacil-

lating, ineffective Assembly of his neighboring province.
Peopled, according to his way of thinking, by runaway
slaves or servants who had fled before their term expired,
and by the most degenerate free white element, this country represented the antithesis of everything admirable in
Virginia and English society. Its inhabitants had no interest in the church, ignored the conventions of marriage
by a minister, allowed their children to go unchristened,
and, worst of all, chose as their legislative representatives
men who were as ignorant and short-sighted as themselves.
It never occurred to Byrd that beneath all this wretchedness and squalor smouldered a love for freedom and independence quite as strong as his own.

When peace with the Indians was definitely concluded
in the autumn of 1713, considerable good will ensued between the Virginia Councillors and their Governor. Spotswood was regarded as having played a major rôle in effect-
ing the matter, and the Council selected Byrd and William
Cocke to draw up an address complimenting him upon his
remarkable diplomacy and wisdom.[27] Spotswood's first
three years of administration, in short, had constituted a
period of unbroken harmony in domestic affairs. But one
is led to suspect that this condition was due in part to the
completeness with which outside concerns had absorbed
him. As soon as they were disposed of, he turned his attention to matters internal, and Byrd was among the first of
the gentlemen with whom he came into violent opposition.

Spotswood made up his mind that the royal quit-rent
revenue should be collected more efficiently. These land
taxes, amounting to two shillings per one hundred acres
annually or that equivalent in tobacco, were all paid to

Byrd as Receiver-General. Byrd did none of the collecting himself. He had the work looked after by the sheriffs of each county, through their deputies. The sheriffs, in turn, settled with him.

But the Governor complained that, in passing through so many indifferently honest hands, this income suffered grave reductions. In the handling of it, he wrote, 'there is the greatest mismanagements and most fraudulent collections there ever were known in a revenue.'[28] He admitted the sheriffs to be the 'gent. of the country,' but their deputies were invariably 'those who would pay most for the privileges of the office.'

In 1713, when the dispute first began, Byrd told the Lieutenant-Governor of a new plan of collection he had hit upon. Its major provision called for a group of four deputy receivers who would supervise the work. These men were to be responsible to the Receiver-General and were to make sworn statements of their accounts to the Auditor. The proposal, Byrd declared in the bitterness of controversy, Spotswood received with the scorn that marked his attitude toward all improvements 'lacking the advantage of his own contrivance.'

This much had been done privately. In July, 1714, the Lieutenant-Governor asked Byrd to suggest a better method of collection. Byrd wrote out the one he had recommended the year before. As might have been suspected, Spotswood ignored it altogether and laid before the Assembly a counter-proposition of his own. It required the sheriffs to collect the rents at places appointed by their county courts, not on the land, as was then the practice. These sheriffs were to settle with Byrd at Williamsburg.

If a planter chose to deal with the Receiver-General direct, he was to be accorded the privilege, together with an eight per cent discount.

Essentially, Spotswood's scheme differed from Byrd's in that the latter wanted to reform matters by creating special collectors. Spotswood was content to use the existing machinery, throwing more strain upon its central point, the Receiver-General; for as he wrote the Lords of Trade, he did not conceive it as His Majesty's intention that this important officer should be a mere figurehead whose work was all done by others. Byrd's plan was in keeping with the spirit then prevalent among English office-holders. Spotswood's appears, rather, the product of a thrifty Scotch management that contemplated no sinecures.

Detailed objections and rejoinders by both principals followed hard upon the formal presentation of the two methods. Spotswood finally called for a vote, and his recommendations were all adopted. They proved far more effective. After one annual collection, he declared that 'one third of the crown lands in this colony had this year yielded a greater revenue than the whole did formerly.' [29]

Defeated rather decisively at home in the controversy with the Lieutenant-Governor, Byrd saw fit early in 1715 to take advantage of the leave of absence he had petitioned for successfully two years before, and departed for England. He carried with him a strong feeling of resentment against Spotswood. In London he was received with consideration. The Lords of Trade called him and one Crawley before them on July 15 and 26 to give information in regard to an Indian war then raging in South Carolina.

These two gentlemen, surprisingly enough, blamed the outbreak entirely upon the English Indian traders, and nothing at all unfavorable was said about Spotswood's share in the matter. Led by the Yemassees, they stated, some fifteen thousand natives were on the warpath.[30] Spotswood had already sent one hundred and fifty men against them and was preparing to dispatch fifty more. Crawley further declared that he had himself seen these traders take hogs, poultry, corn, and other provisions from the Yemassees, paying for them only what they thought fit. And if the Indians 'offered to scruple,' they frequently were beaten or otherwise abused. He said also that he had heard how these same merchants often debauched the Indians' wives and daughters, and, if the women refused to consent, 'they proceed so far as to force them.'

Yet the subject of quit-rents came up the following month, as one might have expected. Byrd was acting on this occasion as agent for the Virginia Assembly. This office had been restored, and by way of reëstablishing himself in the good graces of his countrymen, he went actively to work for them. The specific object of the memorial he presented the Lords of Trade on August 15 was to prevent the revenue from this rent being taken over into the English Treasury. The matter was causing much concern back home, since the new sovereign, George I, contemplated converting the fund into uses of his own as soon as it was collected. The old way had been to leave it in the colony until it reached a considerable sum, subject to the King's orders.

In his memorial Byrd explained that the government of Virginia was maintained by two distinct revenues. There was the two shillings per hogshead tax upon all tobacco exported, which yielded ordinarily three thousand pounds a year. The second source of income was the quit-rents, amounting annually to something between twelve hundred and fifteen hundred pounds.[31] Now, since the expenses of government over a similar period aggregated about thirty-five hundred pounds, this quit-rent fund was looked upon as a surplus to meet the shortage from the tobacco tax. The remainder served for such emergencies as foreign invasions or Indian raids.

As there was no instance of another colony's surplus being transferred to the British Exchequer as soon as collected, 'thus leaving the colony itself naked and defenseless against danger,' Byrd implored the Lords of Trade to recommend that this money be left entirely to the use of Virginia, as its Assembly saw fit. Spotswood could not be so indifferent to the planters' interests as not to desire the success of Byrd's agency. But he said, when delivering his opinion to the Lords of Trade, that he hoped they would accede in the matter expressly in response to his own request, not to that of the Assembly or its spokesman.[32] He was fighting for the same principle this body itself had acted upon in 1703 when it deprived Byrd of his position as agent for the colony — that the proper person to transmit grievances of His Majesty's subjects to England was the Governor or Lieutenant-Governor, who alone as the King's representative could be held accountable for failure to do so in the mother country.

Such an attitude was eminently sane. But the Virginians, quite as sanely, never trusted a Governor so far as to believe he would present their case as well as might an independent retainer of their own. After due deliberation on the quit-rent question, the Lords of Trade decided in Byrd's favor that the surplus should be left in the colonial treasury, but that such a concession was not to be construed as a warrant for extravagant expenditures.

Byrd's success in this affair gratified him extremely. He next began a serious opposition to two laws Spotswood had helped pass in 1714. One of these provided for the payment of debts in tobacco. The other countenanced the formation of a company that should have an exclusive right to all Indian trade. Spotswood vigorously defended both enactments, especially the latter, but Byrd had in his favor the Englishman's hatred of monopoly. In 1717 they were repealed.[33]

This Assembly Agent was obviously becoming very much of a pest to the Governor. Byrd seemed well aware of the fact, and in 1716, that his work might be done without official hindrance, he resigned the Receiver-Generalship. As a royal collector it was unseemly for him to oppose Spotswood, the King's representative, except in a spirit of humility, and of this spirit he had very little. He wrote Custis, in October, saying that he had sold the office for five hundred pounds to James Roscowe, the first person he met who was willing to pay his price. This was not because he feared being removed, but because the place was a burden under existing conditions. To keep it gave Spotswood the opportunity to charge him with misconduct and to get thereby the credit of being zealous in the royal interest. It meant, as he phrased it, that the holder 'must either be a slave to the Lieutenant-Governor's humor, must fawn upon him, jump over a stick whenever he is bid, or else he must have so much trouble loaded on him as to make his place uneasy. In short a man must be either his dog or his ass, neither of which stations suits in the least with my constitution.' [34]

<h1 style="text-align:center">3</h1>

But this period of considerable professional success was abruptly halted by an event which brought with it a sad change in Byrd's domestic affairs. In London he had felt a certain loneliness without his wife, and when he learned that his stay was to be longer than at first seemed probable, he sent for her to come over. She arrived in the summer or fall of 1716, bringing with her their youngest daughter Wilhelmina, then less than a year old. But the trip was ill-fated for Mrs. Byrd. In December she died of smallpox. Byrd told Custis of his misfortune in a note of December 12:

When I wrote you last I little expected that I should be forced to tell you the very melancholy news of my dear Lucy's death, by the same cruel distemper that destroyed her sister. She was taken with an insupportable pain in her head. The doctor soon discovered the ailment to be smallpox, and we thought it best to tell her the danger. She received the news without the least fright and was persuaded she would live until the day she died which happened in twelve hours from the time she was taken. Gracious God, what pains did she take to make a voyage hither to seek a grave! No stranger ever met with more respect in a strange country than she had done here from many persons of distinction, who all pronounced her an honor to Virginia. Alas! how proud was I of her and how severely am I punished for it. But I can dwell no longer upon so afflicting a subject, much less can I think of anything else, therefore, I can

only recommend myself to your pity, and am, as much as anyone can be, dear brother, your most affectionate and humble
servant,

W. Byrd [35]

The death of a parent or wife is not often a matter of
sufficient weight to alter a man outwardly to any marked
extent. There still remain the daily routine of business, the
petty occupations of hour succeeding hour, to make one
number even the strongest attachments among things that
are but half-remembered, or to question them at length as
ever having been at all. Yet one cannot doubt that Byrd,
thoroughly contented in his home, found life depressing
and empty after his loss. It meant that suddenly he must
look after his two children alone, and later that he must
again assume the rôle of a gallant and dally with women at
the silly, vapid business of eighteenth-century courtship.
For he was still comparatively young and found it impossible to conceive of his married life as permanently at an
end.

VI

DISSIDENT COUNCILLOR

He insisted more especially that both the peace and quiet of Virginia depended upon the removal 'of that implacable gentleman Byrd.' This is that same Byrd, he adds, 'who fled with his books for fear of an inquiry.'

I

WHILE Byrd was fairly at odds with Spotswood in England, laboring more seriously than he had ever labored before to hinder such great administrative powers as his opponent claimed 'from being lodged in any bashaw,' there had arisen in Virginia a fresh difference between the Lieutenant-Governor and Council. The dispute brought this body down upon their King's representative almost unanimously. As has been seen, the highest court in the colony was the General Court; and a law of 1705, following one of earlier date, enacted that it should consist of the Governor and Council.[1] Yet in 1699, in order to convict a number of pirates, it had also decreed that 'the commander-in-chief of the colony is hereby desired and impowered to issue out commissions of oyer and terminer under his hand directed to admiralty judges and to such other substantial persons as he shall think fit to appoint.'[2]

When Spotswood first came to Virginia, he saw plainly enough that holding the Supreme Court gave Councillors a vast deal of power. Accordingly, by basing his claim for the privilege upon the law of 1699 and the fact that six members of the Council were of one family, he got his first Assembly to affirm that no former enactments were to be construed as abrogating the King's prerogative to form special courts of oyer and terminer.

This was in 1710. His objections to relatives serving as judges in a case possibly involving their own interest was well founded. But there was a weakness in his position, due to the fact that the appointing of these particular judges was left to himself. And if there was any good reason that the advisory part of the executive should not engross the judicial function, there was better reason that the presiding part of it should not do so. What the colony needed but never obtained was a supreme court, distinct from all other departments of government.

In December, 1712, a man was to be tried for his life, and the Governor, believing he could count on only four of the Council to sit, joined with them the Speaker and 'two other of the most eminent members of the House of Burgesses.'[3] He intended for them to hold the court of oyer and terminer that would hear the case.

But the Councillors refused to serve, contending that the judges should be taken only from their own group. Spotswood dropped the matter for a time, but submitted his case to the Lords of Trade. He insisted upon his right to the authority in question and thought that occasionally it should be exercised, if for no other reason than to establish a respect for the royal prerogative. On June 1, 1716, the Lords, returning to the subject, wrote that he had the right to appoint such courts, unless there was a colonial law to the contrary.[4] That there was no such law, the act he had wisely got passed in 1710 clearly shows.

The decision pleased Spotswood, and, as there were some criminal cases to be disposed of, he appointed for the pur-

pose a special court of oyer and terminer consisting of five
Councillors and four other persons. Only one of the former
number was willing to serve. He was perhaps that same
William Cocke whom Byrd pronounced 'a mere creature
of the Lieutenant-Governor.' [5] There was such an ominous
look on the face of the whole affair that Spotswood hur-
riedly dispatched to England an explanation of his side in
the matter. He was fearful, he declared, lest his enemies
might send over a secret remonstrance 'to private agents,
to be used for concealed designs' [6] — an allusion to Byrd
unquestionably.

The Council was this time unmistakably aroused. Its
members saw in the present step the incipiency of a formid-
able attack on one of their strongest positions. Eight of
them signed a petition against the Lieutenant-Governor's
scheme and sent it to the Lords of Trade. Byrd received
the news joyfully. 'I am glad to find,' he wrote Ludwell,
'that the Council is fairly engaged with the Lieutenant-
Governor. They have a good cause and I hope I shall be
able to procure justice to be done to them.' [7]

It was true, he added, by way of putting himself thoroughly in accord with his fellows, that he had once proposed the establishment of a supreme court in the colony,
differentiated from the Council. But he had shown his
plan to no one except the Lord Justice, who approved of
it. His only intent in the matter had been to obviate the
absurdity of allowing men who knew no law, as frequently
happened under the present arrangement, to sit at law
cases. Yet, at that, he had favored leaving all chancery
jurisdiction to the Councillors. This would have enabled
them to retain their salary, then amounting to three hun-

dred and fifty pounds a year. He had thought, too, that
it would be well to have the quit-rents paid out in salaries
to the judges, who would spend it in Virginia, and that it
would also be a good thing because it would encourage his
countrymen to bring up their sons to be lawyers. These
were his true reasons, 'and not the mean prospect of being
one of the judges myself.' But since his colleagues, by
opposing the oyer and terminer courts, seemed hostile to
his plan, he assured Ludwell that he would by no means
urge its adoption any longer.

Up to this time Byrd had had free access to the Lords
of Trade, but now that body, influenced no doubt by
Spotswood's reference to 'private agents,' objected to receiving further addresses through him. He insisted that
as one of the Council he should be heard in a matter affect-
ing his fellow members and himself so vitally. On this
ground they told him he might appear. But he wrote Ludwell again that the Assembly ought to have an agent of its
own, since Blackiston, who had been appointed by the
Council, was in the Lieutenant-Governor's influence. The
Assembly met in the spring of 1718 and elected Byrd to
this office. Spotswood vetoed the bill. But when the Burgesses resolved to pay his salary themselves, Byrd forthwith began to discharge his new duties.

The brief address he delivered before the Lords of Trade
on the subject of oyer and terminer courts is as fine and
eloquent a document as Byrd ever wrote:

The great diligence your Lordships employ to rectify whatever you find amiss in the plantations encourages me to lay before you an unhappy difference betwixt the governor and the
Council of Virginia, on occasion of his having joined several

persons with the Council in a commission of oyer and terminer, which I humbly conceive he could not regularly do, for the following reasons:

1. The laws of that colony, and particularly the twenty-fourth in the printed book, have most expressly limited the trials of life and limb to the general court, and until such laws be repealed, either by subsequent acts or by His Majesty's proclamation, I humbly conceive they are binding against all governors whatever.

2. King Charles the second, by his royal charter, bearing date of the 10 of October, 1676, was graciously pleased to grant amongst other privileges to that colony that the governor and the Council for the time being should have full power and authority to hear and to determine (the very English of oyer and terminer) all treasons, murders, felonys, etc. to be committed within that government. Now if they were to hear and determine all pleas of the crown, there can be no room for the Lieutenant-Governor to constitute any other judges for that purpose.

3. All criminal cases have, by the common usage of that colony since its first settlement, been heard and determined by the governor and council for the time being. A custom, therefore, established by so long practice, and to which no matter of inconvenience has ever been objected, ought not in reason or justice to be overturned to gratify the humor, or perhaps the passion, of any governor.

4. The custom consigning all trials in criminal cases to the governor and council hath been founded on reason and justice, because as nobody must doubt the governor's being well-qualified; so likewise the Council is by His Majesty's express instruction to be appointed out of the gentlemen of the greatest ability and best estates in the country, who are certainly most capable and most likely to do impartial justice betwixt His Majesty and all his subjects. Besides, the Councillors are always appointed by the king himself whereas the persons joined to them in these commissions of oyer and terminer are only named by

the Lieutenant-Governor without the advice of anybody, for a particular time and (it may easily happen) for a particular purpose.

5. To the foregoing reasons may be added the very fatal inconvenience that may follow upon the putting it into the sole power of a governor to try any person by what judges he may think most proper. Whoever has had the fortune to live in the plantations has abundant reason to know that governors are not in the least exempt from human frailty, such as a passionate love for money, resentment against such as presume to oppose their designs, partiality to their creatures and favorites, and many other passions to which men in power are more subject than other people. Now supposing this to be true, I must humbly submit to your lordships whether a governor will not have it too much in his power, either to condemn the innocent or acquit the guilty, if he have the sole authority of appointing his judges; or whether it be reasonable that a governor who by a most plain instruction can't appoint so much as a Justice of the Peace to decide the smallest property, without the advice of the Council, should yet take upon him by his own absolute will and pleasure, without any advice in the world, to appoint judges who without appeal are to determine not only concerning the lives and liberties but also regarding the whole estates of all those unhappy persons who shall be brought before them...

Upon the whole matter, in regard to that this step of the Lieutenant-Governor has been made contrary to the express terms of the royal charter, in violation of the laws of that colony and against a constant usage founded on reason and justice, and since such fatal inconveniences may attend the Governor's being invested with so absolute a power, from which no advantage may accrue to His Majesty, I take no doubt but your lordships will please to give such directions as may put a stop to this innovation and prevent its being drawn into a precedent for the future—lest that which was graciously intended by His Majesty for a privilege and advantage to the good inhabitants of that colony may be turned to their apparent danger and oppression.

I have the honor to be, with the greatest respect in the world, My Lords, your Lordships

Most obedient, humble servant,
W. Byrd [8]

Nowhere has the true source of this difference been more ably expressed. The struggle was one between colonial self-government and imperial control, between rule based upon custom, charter, and royal restrictions, on the one hand, and upon arbitrary domination on the other. Here, in germ, were the principles of the Revolution of 1776. The thing that retarded physical resistance was the fact that only the Councillors seemed concerned with the point disputed. The yeomanry lacked both class consciousness and a sense of political equality.

Yet in Spotswood's behalf it should be said that he was hampered by the same difficulty that weighed upon the endeavors of every loyal representative who wished to advance the welfare of his charge: it was impossible to reconcile the demands of prerogative with the expanding energies of a state essentially democratic.[9] But Byrd's attitude, at this date, was quite untenable. The entire tradition of the Lords of Trade was bent upon maintaining the Crown's power of ultimate authority. This body existed for the purpose of checking just such instances of usurpation as were here being considered. It was plain, to its members, that the case was one of the Council's delegating to itself a function the exclusiveness of which had been manifestly denied by the Act of 1710.

Byrd, truly enough, used his eloquence with consummate skill. Yet he did not mention the above law at all until a decision of the Attorney-General, to whom the case

was referred, forced him to shift his position considerably.
This authority declared that the Governor did have the
power Byrd had denied he possessed, but advised that it
be sparingly used.[10] Byrd then took the matter to the
Crown, though by this time he was forced to admit the
truth of the Attorney-General's decision and could only
petition His Majesty that Spotswood be enjoined not to
exercise the privilege except on rare occasions.

But even this boon was denied him. When the Lords of
Trade presented both sides to the King, they added an
obviously disastrous statement to their report. The application against the Governor's using this power, they declared, 'does not come from the people of the colony, but
only from those persons who would engross the privilege
for themselves of being sole judges in all criminal causes,
so that it seems rather a claim of power for themselves, to
the prejudice of His Majesty's prerogative. And as there
may be great inconveniences in confining the power entirely
to the Council, and as the governor will be answerable for
any abuse he might make of such power, their lordships
humbly recommend that it may remain as it is at present,
by His Majesty's commission in the hands of the governor.'[11] In the face of this strong opinion, Byrd was
baffled. His appeal came to naught.

In the meantime Spotswood was making life unpleasant
for the Councillors in Virginia. He had learned that in an
address which eight of them sent to Byrd, he had been
charged with introducing into the government 'new
measures of dangerous consequences.' On the morning of
March 12, 1718, when five of these eight subscribers were
present, he brought this statement to their notice and

demanded that they point out what new measures he had proposed. His accusers were somewhat confused and asked that the matter be postponed until a later meeting, when all of the eight signatories would be present. Spotswood replied that he would have thought an hour long enough to remember at least one of his innovations, but that he would give them the time desired.[12]

On March 31, seven were in attendance, and they gave as an answer that they did not think it proper for the Lieutenant-Governor 'to have meddled with that letter without their lordships' permission.' Spotswood, it seems, had found out the contents of the message the Councillors directed to Byrd. Their resentment was increased, they added, by reason of the fact that peace negotiations between the factions had been in progress for some time. Spotswood replied that he knew all this, but that his opponents were unwilling to accept the proposals of truce already made. He then ordered it entered in the minutes that he had called the Councillors for specifications of the charges and got none, and that he concluded they could give none.

The Lieutenant-Governor was to have one more chance to humble the pride of his opponents. On May 14 he appeared in Council with the Attorney-General's opinion regarding oyer and terminer. He had the document read and then asked whether the Councillors now conceded that the Governor had the power of constituting these judges, with or without their assistance. 'Upon which the said gentlemen declared that they acquiesced in the determination of the Lords Commissioners of Trade.' Yet when he next appointed a court of this nature, he announced that he should name Councillors only. But he required each publicly to acknowledge that he sat by virtue of Spotswood's preference, not because of his membership in the upper house.[13] The controversy was at an end. It marked a decisive victory for the king's representative.

In England, Byrd likewise felt the effects of his retainers' defeat. A letter from Harrison to Ludwell shows that his influence was waning. 'I consider,' said he, 'the consequences if Collo. Byrd should ever obtain his end and come here governor, and we should be so unfortunate as to differ with him. Now that Colo. Byrd will come here in that station I have every reason to think and therefore we should act so as not to give him any advantage against us by which he might keep us in awe.' [14]

If Byrd really did have such an ambition in mind, it was destined, like so many other of his later plans, to disappointment. But one suspects, in view of the Lieutenant-Governor's action after he had humbled his opponents in the oyer and terminer controversy, that Byrd was much too busy attempting to hold his seat in the Council to hope for anything more.

For on the first of July, 1718, Spotswood requested, in a letter to his superior, the Earl of Orkney, that four of the 'most turbulent' Council members, Blair, Ludwell, Smith, and Byrd, be removed.[15] Orkney appeared before the Lords of Trade the following month and proposed an investigation.[16] They put off any action for a while, but Spotswood wrote again urging that Byrd in particular be unseated on account of his long absence from the colony.[17] The following February he insisted more especially that both the peace and the quiet of Virginia depended upon the dismissal 'of that implacable gentleman Byrd.' He calls out complaints, 'no matter if true or false,' and expects with reports about a tottering Governor to gain his ends and have that Governor displaced. This is that same Byrd, he adds, 'who fled with his books for fear of an inquiry.' [18]

The Lords of Trade were by this time completely won over. And though Byrd had two months before asked for a copy of the accusations against him, 'together with the common liberty of justifying myself,' [19] they recommended on February 24 that Mr. Cole Digges be made a Councillor in his place. There was now nothing left for the proud Templar to do but humble himself. It was possibly as painful a gesture as he ever made, but he went through with it.

'To convince their Lordships that he is sincerely in-clined to peace,' he wrote this body on March 24, 'he promises to employ all the credit he has with the Council to dispose them to a sincere pacification upon the terms of the Lieutenant-Governor's own plan, but to do this good work effectually he begs their Lordships to prepare the way by writing letters both to the Lieutenant-Governor and Council on the several points he especially refers to.' If this be done, 'he doubts not to see in a little time by these methods an entire harmony established in that colony.' [20]

The Assembly was also making overtures toward a reconciliation, and Orkney seconded their action. The Lords yielded to such an extent that on April 8 they re-commended Digges for the Council 'in the room of Edmund Berkeley, deceased'; but, as if to keep Byrd still in awe, they suggested that Peter Beverley be given his place.[21]

In June the question of his removal came up before the Privy Council at the Court of Saint James's. In his defense Byrd set forth that for many years he had been a member of the Council; that about five years before, being Receiver-General of His Majesty's revenue, he obtained leave from the Commissioners of the Treasury to come to England; that the leave was seen and approved by Spotswood at that time, and that several unavoidable accidents had prevented his return. The Lords of the Privy Council then, 'upon consideration of Byrd's long service and that he hath engaged to return with the first shipping to Virginia, agree humbly to recommend him to His Majesty's favor for his continuance in the said Council, and that if the Lieutenant-Governor shall have suspended or dismissed him from the said place, he shall be required immediately to restore him, as likewise his former rank therein.' [22]

When His Majesty signed his approval to the recommendation of the Privy Council, Byrd was doubtless a highly pleased person. If he had ever trembled on the brink of a precipitation into political disaster, it was during the latter months of this controversy. It is difficult to imagine what would have become of him had he really lost his position. Always a man of the most dominant pride, he would have found it almost inconceivable to return to Virginia stripped of his honors. Yet it is hardly to be doubted that it was by virtue of his being among the most influential residents of his colony that he was enabled to hold the esteem of his wealthy English friends. The case

was one of a new-world leader, well groomed in the traditions of the mother country, meeting the more important
men thereof upon the common ground of eminence. This
made the most desirable social contacts easy to a person-
able individual who, like Byrd, felt inclined to take advantage of them. But at his age, the permanent loss of his
position as Councillor would probably have been attended
by a gradual decline in prominence in London and, with
estates growing ever larger in the colony, by eventual
near-obscurity there also.

Byrd fulfilled his promise to reconcile the differences in
Virginia. He arrived there about the first of January,
1720, and the Council minutes for the following April 29th
record that

Whereas divers disputes and controversys have heretofore arisen
between His Majesty's Lieutenant-Governor and some of the
Council, occasioned by a difference in opinion in matters relating to the administration of the government, both parties
heartily inclining to put a period to all past contentions as well
as to prevent any future discords which may happen of the like
nature, have this day mutually agreed that all past controversys
of what kind soever be forever buried in oblivion, and that there
may be hereafter no other contention than who shall most
promote the King's service and the public benefit of the
colony.

It was also decided that future disputes should be referred to England for adjustment. In informing the Lords
of Trade of the matter, the Council's statement declared
that all points were 'fully compromised, to their own very
great satisfaction and to the universal joy of the country.' [23] This reconciliation was considerably simplified by

Spotswood's not having suspended Byrd from his seat before he reached home.

The final difference between Byrd and the Lieutenant-Governor did not amount to much. Byrd really figured in the matter only as the agent around whom the dispute raged — this time with the Burgesses in the rôle of Spotswood's opponent. That body, in December, 1720, desired an independent agent who would represent to the King their actions 'in an affair relating to a treaty with the five nations of Indians at Albany and all such matters as may hereafter be agreed upon.' [24] They chose Byrd for the office and advocated a disbursement of four hundred pounds to pay his expenses.

It was of course necessary, in a case of this sort, that the upper house approve the appropriation involved. When the question came up before the Councillors, the Governor absented himself. But he sent in a long address in which he again contended that he was the proper medium through which all 'occurrences' in the colony were to be transmitted to England. 'And in no case am I directed to allow the General Assembly to interpose a person of their own creation; nay, the late Queen as well as his present Majesty have markedly discouraged such attempts.' [25] 'However,' he added, 'if you continue desirous that Mr. Byrd when he goes home should solicit some certain matters in behalf of this government, I will agree thereto, provided he receive all his instructions from me, and will enter into strict bond not to meddle with any other affair of this government.'

But the Burgesses knew Byrd's temper well enough to feel certain that he would accept no office whatever under such haughty restrictions. When the substance of this communication was delivered to them, they pleaded 'an entire ignorance of any other affairs by him intended to be meddled with,' and 'hoped the Governor would not deprive the country of a person so capable and in all respects most proper for his employment by insisting on the proposed amendment to our resolve, which, if added, we have just reason to believe, will prevent his engaging in that service for his country.' [26]

A joint committee from the two houses thereupon was sent to Spotswood to learn his decision in the matter. He consented, and thus for the third time Byrd was made an agent for the Assembly in England. Yet it is probable that in this instance he would not have accepted the place had he not previously signified his intention of returning to London [27] and found himself rather badly in need of money to defray the expenses of the trip. For to term his past five years of arduous contention in behalf of liberty by such an unceremonious epithet as 'meddling' was little short of an insult. Like most insults, however, this one perhaps did not lack entirely an element of truth.

VII

RELUCTANT PILGRIM

How could such unrealities as time and distance blight the strongest attachments, the truest friendships? How could life run so utterly between one's fingers to the ground, never to be retrieved? A belated Cavalier in far-away Virginia, he wondered, remembering the past, the days that could be no more, hid in
death's dateless night.

I

CERTAINLY the breast of a man in love is like the troubled sea
that never, never rests. It heaves and swells alike, tossed and
disturbed by sighs instead of storms. When the wretch's heart
beats high and is big with hopes of happiness, how it resembles
the waves that roll aloft and seem to raise their saucy pride to
heaven. But when they fall again and humbly retire into the
bosom of the deep, they represent the lover's fears and sink his
spirit into despair. Oh that the good-natured Charmante would
please to figure for herself the restlessness of such an unhappy
man and pity me. What heavenly scenes has Hope sometimes
opened to my eyes when your dear smiles seemed to promise all
that was delightful in this world. And then, alas! by a turn as
sudden and unaccountable as those that happen in the air, my
bliss was overcast by your frowns and a dreadful gloom has shut
in all the pleasing prospect. Oh, let that gloom clear up again, I
conjure you, Madam, and speak peace to a troubled soul.[1]

The autumn of 1722 has come, and Byrd, it may be
easily surmised, is very much in love. The fact is scarcely
propitious. He is well into his forty-ninth year and playing
at a game that, with all his grace and culture, he has never
quite been able to master. Now, too, he must play it with
a younger generation, and a strange lot they are surely,

marrying, they avow, for love only, sometimes even when the union brings poverty of the vilest sort.

Byrd hardly considered himself a middle-aged man. His health was good. He had kept himself constantly active at one thing or another, riding about his plantations in Virginia, overseeing his overseers, or busying himself if in London with colony affairs or the city's engaging social life. Yet to many an attractive lady of George I's reign he was perhaps becoming a bit old-fashioned. There were more romantically exciting hours to be spent in the company of younger gallants who were not so anxious to become serious and ask one to forego the many delights of England for what was, after all, a raw lifeless country by comparison.

The situation reflects scant credit upon these eighteenth-century belles, to be sure. Byrd was still reasonably eligible and by all means as pleasantly disposed a companion as any sensible female could wish. But youth seems frequently irrational in such matters, especially when the choice lies between men of markedly different years. In this instance it happened that almost from the start Charmante began to discourage her distinguished planter-suitor in the interests of a quite ordinary rival.

It was not Byrd's first lost cause, though, one should remember, and he rarely gave up without a struggle. Besides, he continues,

What hope is there of getting the better of a passion which even absence influences? Should I run about to places of diversion, I should only find out how infinitely better pleased I should be in your delightful company. What though I should converse with other ladies, they will only convince me how much your excellencies outshine theirs. Nothing can be done to make me love you less. It is not in nature, it is impossible, it is now alas! too late. Thus Madam I am fated by invincible necessity to be entirely and unalterably yours. I entreat you therefore, if you have any pity, any compassion, smile upon my inclinations and bless me with your favor.[2]

Two nights later he dreamed an elaborate dream.

As I went to sleep as I constantly do with my dearest Charmante in my thoughts [he wrote his lady] I fancied I saw her in a shady grove sitting on a mossy bank in pensive posture, with her head reclined upon her hand. At my approach she started up with some marks of surprise and discomposure. Her face beamed lovely as a cherubim, her stature just, her shape proportionable and constrained, and her behavior perfectly graceful and engaging. Her dress was neat and light and well fashioned, which added new beauty to her person. I addressed this divine creature with wonder, counting over every visible perfection, but when I heard her speak and observed the good nature which sat smiling upon every feature, I was so struck with the charms of her mind that I forgot those of the body.

For some time she seemed to listen to my tender tale with patience and, I hoped, with pity. But on a sudden the wind changed, she grew surprisingly reserved, and seemed uneasy at my presence. Grieved to the soul, I instantly retired with all the anguish of a slighted lover, hoping my absence might deliver my cruel charmer from a wretch who was disagreeable to her. Alas! instead of being abated by keeping away, the distemper increased the impression every day and seemed to be the last thing that would die of me.[3]

But Byrd's dream anguish was soon relieved by a most delightful pageant.

At some distance [he continues] I heard a flourish of trumpets, hautbos and kettle drums; and drawing my eyes towards it, I

perceived a fine procession advancing. The first person that
appeared was a grave gentleman with a countenance very composed, holding in his hand a lighted flambeau made of wax. Next
to him rode Venus in her golden car drawn by two innocent
turtles which billed and cooed as they passed along. The goddess
looked all the while over her shoulder and smiled upon Charmante, who followed next the car, reaching out to her the cestus
full of all the enchantments of her sex. She was clothed in a
loose robe of spotless white with her sable tresses flowing in ring-
lets upon her shoulders. Thus adorned, she seemed to rival the
goddess so much that the wanton cupids left their mother to
frisk and play about her.[4]

It was the frisking cupids, he went on to explain, who
finally came to him and led him to the fair Charmante,
telling him the while that from all mankind he had been
chosen to accompany her in this blessed procession.

They were auspiciously chaperoned.

On the right hand of my dear angel walked a comely dame
with a calm and steady countenance in a mantle of deepest azure
leading with her left hand a dog that fixed his eyes wistfully upon
her and wagged his tail. And upon my left marched a beautiful
virgin without any airs or ornament in the world. All she had on
was a lawn slip through which might be discerned very comely
proportions. Next to us followed a matron with a serene and
peaceable countenance having an everlasting smile upon her face
and pointing up to heaven. After her came a plump damsel but
very cheerful and good mannered, pouring out of a cornucopia
the finest fruit and gayest flowers in plenty and perfection.

This stately *entourage* was made complete by a little flower
girl and by two boys carrying mitres.

In this order we marched to the temple of honor where a digni-
fied priest joined our hands and descending angels sang Amen,
in celestial notes. Adieu, my dear Charmante — may you be

as happy all your life long as I was during the few moments of this delightful dream.[5]

Yet the blisses of this imaginary world were to find no counterpart in reality. For the next two days, it should be admitted, Charmante was laid up 'with a swelled face and cold which,' Byrd could not resist saying, 'I fear you have caught by the excess of care you take of yourself.' [6] But a week later, the entire affair was rudely and abruptly terminated.

It appears that Charmante had fully recovered and, while in the company of some other gentleman at an extremely public place, possibly the theater, she chanced upon Byrd and proceeded to display her ill manners so far as to request that he discontinue his unwelcome attentions entirely. To Byrd the situation was, naturally enough, unique. The idea of a civilized lady thus utterly ignoring the proprieties of decency left him — as it would leave almost any gentleman — speechless. It was not until the following morning that he recovered sufficiently to write her a last note. But at no time in all his life did he ever appear more consummately the gentleman:

London, November 7, 1722

I beg the generous Charmante will forgive me if I presume to write once more and that she won't look upon that to be a transgression of her orders which is only a promise of obedience. Though I must confess her last orders were very short and sullen, yet I will prove the entire regard I have for her by entirely observing them. I will not endeavor to convince her that the slightest hint of her pleasure shall be a law to me, though never so disagreeable to myself. But, dear Madam, what could provoke you to deliver your commands to me in that odd place? I don't remember I was asking an alms of you that you should

deny me, like a common beggar, in the street. You know very
well you have lately had more opportunity than one of signifying
your mind to me at your own house. That certainly had been a
more proper place unless you intended, by the surprise of the on-
set, to cutt off all possibility of reply. Surely you could not ap-
prehend I should in the bitterness of my soul have reproached
you with any instances of your former conduct in case you had
attacked me in a fair field of battle.... During my whole address
to you I have behaved with truth and honor, and I shall always
love you too well to do or say anything to your disadvantage.
However, if after all you should determine to make me unhappy,
I will submit to my hard fate without reproaching anything but
my stars and in return of your unkind usage shall earnestly pray
that everything that is good, everything that is prosperous may
befall you. And if ever you should marry any other man, may he
set as just a value upon your fine qualities and charming person
and take as much pleasure in making you hapy as I do; more
I'm sure will be impossible. May sprightly health and gaiety of
mind and all the joys resulting from virtue and honor attend you
to the end of your days. Provided my dearest Charmante is thus
completely blessed, it matters not what becomes of her unfortunate humble servant.

W. BYRD [7]

Such is all that is known of the affair from Byrd himself,
and Charmante's identity, like Facetia's, is undiscover-
able. But this was not always the case. At least one member of a more recent Byrd generation was aware of many
of the suppressed details and defended her distinguished
ancestor with some tartness. Writing about 1865 and
evidently relying upon family traditions, Miss Elizabeth
Byrd Nicholas tells us that these

passionate billets [the Charmante correspondence] were writ to a
lady who had more charms than honor, more wit than discretion.
In the beginning she gave the writer of them the plainest marks

of her favor. He did not hint his passion to her but spoke it openly and confirmed it with many a tender squeeze of the hand, which she suffered with the patience of a martyr. She saw him every day, received his letters, and fed the flame by the gentlest behaviour in the world 'till at last of a sudden, without any provocation on his part, she grew *resty* and in a moment turned all her smiles into frowns and all his hopes into despair.

Whether this sudden change was caused by private scandal she had received about him or from pure inconsistency of temper, he can't be sure. The first is not unlikely, for he had a rival who had no hopes of succeeding openly and therefore it might be necessary to work under ground and blow him by a mine. This suspicion is confirmed a little by the rival's marrying her afterwards. He was then poor, and 'tis likely the good natured woman might have wed him out of charity — especially as at that time he was so unhealthy that he stood more in need of a nurse than a wife. She did not choose him for his beauty and length of chin, though possibly she might for those pure morals which recommended him to his grace of W—— for a companion. But if after all she did not marry him for his virtue either, then it must have been for the worst quality any hus—...[8]

What it was that to a mid-Victorian spinster constituted the worst quality any husband could possess one is left to conjecture, for the manuscript at this point becomes illegible. Yet it is hardly being more than fair to say that, seen from his letters, Byrd's conduct was entirely admirable, and that he ceased his attentions as graciously as one could ask.

2

It was not long after this time, so tradition has it, that Byrd's eldest daughter Evelyn, now a fine lady of sixteen years, was presented at Court. The tiny fan of carved

Chinese ivory she carried upon this great occasion has long been among the treasured relics of succeeding Byrd generations, its faded tracery suggestive, perhaps, of the frustrated life of its earliest owner. For Evelyn, one is generally told, was actually affianced to the Earl of Petersborough and for love of him (her father having objected to the match) she preferred to live unmarried. Another, less often repeated story names Charles Mordaunt, Petersborough's grandson, as the suitor, attributing his ill-success to his religion, Catholicism. Still another account has it that the Earl himself even followed Byrd home in 1726 and there renewed the proposals upon which the latter frowned.

And as no well authenticated haunt of ancient aristocracy is to be found without its ghost, so Westover traditions tell twilight listeners or groups around the fire at Yuletide how the tap, tap, of Evelyn's high-heeled slippers continues to be heard in the corridors or on the stairs of the home from which, long ago, she faded broken-hearted to the grave.[9]

All of this is delightfully consistent with the canons of romance.

It has thrown an enduring halo around the memory of the fair one whose hand was kissed by my Lords Oxford and Chesterfield, of whom sneering Hervey deigned to approve, who supped with Pope at his Twickenham villa while the town was still ringing with the success of his *Odyssey*, who was noticed by Beau Nash, the autocrat of Bath, who saw Cibber and Mrs. Oldfield play, who read *Gulliver's Travels* as they were first presented to the public by his reverence, the dean of St. Patrick's, and who, from the presence chamber of unroyal royalty, through a society reeking with wine and musk and snuff and scandal, passed back to her plantation home as unblemished as she came.[10]

SALEM COLLEGE LIBRARY
Winston-Salem, North Carolina

The most interesting fact in connection with this supposed affair is that Petersborough at the time was in his sixty-fourth year. All in all he was rather extraordinary. 'How I should have liked seeing that noble old madcap in his boots,' said Thackeray,[11] '(he actually had the audacity to walk about Bath in boots) with his blue ribbon and stars and a cabbage under each arm, and a chicken in each hand which he had been cheapening for dinner.' Hogarth caricatured him upon his knees before the singer Cuzzoni, who draws in his gold pieces with a rake. Horace Walpole's description is more flattering: 'Petersborough,' he wrote, 'was one of those men of careless wit and negligent grace who scatter a thousand *bon mots* and idle verses, which we painful compilers gather and hoard 'till the authors stare to find themselves authors. He was a man, as his friends said, who would neither live nor die like any other mortal.' In one of his characteristic letters, written to Pope, he gave a suggestion of his views upon womankind:

You seem to think it vexatious that I should allow you but one woman at a time to praise or love. If I dispute with you upon this point, I doubt every jury will give a verdict against me. So, sir, with a Mahometan indulgence, I allow you pluralities, the favorite privilege of your church.... I find you don't mend upon correction. Again I must tell you you must not think of women in a reasonable way.[12]

The Earl wrote his memoirs shortly before his death. If his widow, the singer Anastasia Robinson '(whom he married in 1724 and acknowledged as his wife ten years later)' had not destroyed them, all question of Evelyn's fascination for this dissolute but gallant old warrior could, perhaps, be settled with certainty. It is said that in this work he confessed to three capital crimes committed before he became of age. He died in 1735, 'laughing and mocking in the intervals of agonizing pain and entertaining a company of ten at dinner immediately before the end.' [13]

But the whole story of her love appears incredible from certain letters Byrd wrote Boyle shortly after he returned to the colony. 'My young gentlewomen,' he says, referring to Evelyn and Wilhelmina, 'like everything in the country except the retirement. They can't get the plays, the operas, and the masquerades out of their heads; much less can they forget their friends. But the lightness of the air helps them to bear all their losses with more spirit, and that they may amuse themselves the better they are every day up to their elbows in housewifery.' [14]

The following year he wrote Boyle again about the disadvantages to gallantry in Virginia and how well this conduced to matrimony. This benign state 'thrives so excellently here,' he went on to say, 'that an old maid or an old bachelor is as rare among us and is reckoned as ominous as a blazing star. One of the most antique virgins I am acquainted with is my daughter Evelyn.' She was then twenty-one. 'Either our young fellows are not smart enough for her or she seems too smart for them, but in a little time I hope they will split the difference.' [15]

It thus seems that this young lady, when once she returned to Virginia, was not at all of a disposition that would lead one to imagine her as pining away for an earl of thrice her age. More than likely, as Byrd suggests, she turned out a bit 'too smart' for what eligible suitors she had an opportunity of knowing in the colony. There were few inducements for a girl of this century who loved society to exchange an old-world residence for a new.

Evelyn died in 1737. She was thirty years old. The following acrostic, a work probably of some native suitor who had been refused with gentleness, appeared in the *Virginia Gazette* two weeks after the event:

E ver constant to her friend
V igilant in truth's defense
E ntertaining to her end
L ife! brimful of eloquence.
Y outh in person; age in sense
N ature gave her store immense.

B ut she's fled and is no more
Y onder soars in fields of light!
R obbed of all our little store,
D eath! oh death! we're ruined quite.[16]

3

The summer following his unfortunate affair with Charmante, Byrd was in a strange state of mind. Apparently he was planning to return home and give up risking any further tilts with these vacillating 'resty' London coquettes. One can scarcely blame him for such a resolve. It would have required an optimism little short of heroic to prevent Byrd's feeling a cordial disgust with womankind after one of its choice representatives had made so blatant a display of her rudeness. He wrote his brother-in-law Custis that he had already decided to sail for Virginia in the spring of 1724 [17] and hardly knew how he would be able to abide the departure of his vessel.

But this same letter contained a suspicious admission. Byrd, now in his fiftieth year, discoursed at some length upon the subject of old age. It should be reckoned, he said, not by the time one has lived in the world, but from the decline of one's bodily vigor. As for himself, he was still philosophically a youth. He had the same high spirits, the same zest for living, and (though his treatment at the hands of Charmante had filled him with superficial misgivings in the matter) the same yearning for companionship that he had known when young. These things, unfulfilled, had made the past eight years lonely, amid all the crowded life about him.

They were likewise the things which caused him, some ten months later, to marry again. His second wife was Maria Taylor, daughter and co-heiress of Thomas Taylor of Kensington.[18] At the time of the wedding she was twenty-five years old.

Certain friendships of Byrd traceable to this union are of subsequent importance. Through it he became connected with a family handed down to literary history by the biographers of Pope. A near relative of the Taylors — the exact kinship does not appear — had married Teresa Blount, in whose presence, the poet declared to Gay, he had spent three or four hours a day for more than fifteen years.[19] It is this fact that lends some credence to the story that Evelyn was entertained by Pope at Twickenham. For Patty Blount was quite intimate with the Byrds, and her portrait, done by Kneller, long remained one of the most admired works in the Westover gallery.

A sister of Maria Taylor married Francis Otway, an English army officer who later became Colonel of the

Guards.[20] These two, his sister-in-law and her husband, were perhaps the truest English friends Byrd ever had. Between him and men like Southwell or Boyle there yawned a certain economic disparity never to be quite disregarded. While he was in the company of these notables, or in London, a vivid memory of his engaging personality proved enough to make him eagerly sought after. But in the years following his return to the colony, he was almost forgotten by Boyle and completely so by the Southwells. 'Distance,' he once said, 'they reckon the same as death.' [21]

Byrd could never reconcile himself to the finality of such an attitude. His failure to do so lies back of all the letters he kept writing to his friends abroad. It explains his *History of the Dividing Line* and the many portraits he brought back to Westover. How could such unrealities as time and distance blight the strongest attachments, the truest friendships. How could life run so utterly between one's fingers to the ground, never to be retrieved. A belated Cavalier in far-away Virginia, he wondered, remembering the past, the days that could be no more, hid in death's dateless night....

The reasons inducing Byrd to return to Virginia in the spring of 1726 were distinctly of a financial nature. Less than a year after his marriage he found himself a father again. Once more the expense of a family was becoming considerable. There were Evelyn and Wilhelmina by a first alliance and an infant from the second. For the past five or six years, he also must frequently have remembered, there had been no supplementary income from the office of Assembly Agent; and with tenants upon his plantations paying their tobacco debts less punctually than was required,[22] a personal investigation had become necessary. But he left with the intention of soon returning. It would take possibly five years to straighten out his affairs in the colony. After that he could come back. A peaceful old age in London would follow — free of debt. The thought consoled him. Among his friends he spoke of his departure as a 'pilgrimage to the new world.' [23]

4

Crossing the Atlantic in the early spring of 1726 was both an adventure and an achievement. One traveled, as John Fontaine had done some ten years earlier, at the approximate rate of three to six knots an hour. But such startling progress, of course, presupposed fair weather. If the sailing were rough, as frequently happened, a frail vessel became a victim of the wind's caprice, blown from its course mutilated or in hopeless disrepair. 'Peas as hard as shot for breakfast, two fowls killed by the bad weather for dinner, and stirabout for supper...' [24] taken together on such occasions they were indeed satisfying fare.

Then there were the pirates. Around Cape Charles and Cape Henry, it seemed to travelers, one found them clustering like hornets. In brief, if a man who traveled without a convoy missed the storms, he generally ran amuck a sloop of villains; so that whether a voyage was to require three months or the brief span of five weeks, or whether land would be sighted at all, depended upon factors that few mariners had the temerity to predict.

To a prospective colonist of circumscribed fortune, the inducements to settle in the Old Dominion were few. 'I cannot get a pint of good two penny beer to drink your health,' George Home wrote his brother from Williamsburg,[25] 'for all our drink here is water and sometimes rum, but it is very dear and very little money to buy it.' Clothing and linen were equally expensive, selling, Home continued, at three times their English price. The universal commodity (used for money apart from serving as the only marketable product of importance) was tobacco. The inhabitants were beginning to appear reserved, evincing a certain aloofness toward unimpressive newcomers. 'I find,' Home told his brother, 'that there is nothing to be got here without very good recommendation.' [26] He had to move on to the backwoods.

The economic situation in the colony was indeed sorry. One must go back for an explanation to the year 1660, when, under the Duke of York, the Royal African Company began to compete with the Dutch slave-traders. The newcomers at first met with grave difficulties. Native chieftains were stirred up against them, and two wars had to be fought with Holland before their right to a share in the traffic received acknowledgment.[27]

When the English did firmly establish themselves in this business, in the eighteenth century, a significant change in Virginia plantations inevitably followed. Smaller yeoman landholders who tilled their own ground saw with increasing dismay that the yearly influx of cheap slave labor was soon to drive them out of the tobacco market entirely. The hopelessness of their situation was augmented by the Navigation Laws, which, even under wholly favorable conditions, made any but a reasonable profit impossible. Like George Home, the newcomer, this important middle class, a valuable factor in any population, was being compelled to migrate elsewhere, either into North Carolina or westward beyond the tidewater.

British statesmen of this generation had no conception of their colonies as an extended England. The empire consisted of two distinct parts, mother country and colonial possessions. When their interests conflicted, the latter were at fault. They believed in keeping their unemployed at home and building up domestic industries, rather than in sending them away in quest of work. From the goods they manufactured the colonies were to be supplied.[28]

What could be more desirable? they reasoned. If the finished products were not made in England and brought over at the planter's expense, one half of a voyage would be altogether without profit. Besides, the spirit of freedom, already strong enough, would make their dependencies unmanageable were they to establish factories of their own. Such a policy, by the time of Byrd's return, had transformed Virginia into a one-crop squirearchy, wherein only men of extensive estates could hold their own against the ever-increasing employment of slaves and the constant price fluctuations of their sole commodity, tobacco.

Yet the country was far from settled. Wolves wandered about the scattered plantations so dangerously numerous on winter nights that county courts gave rewards of one hundred pounds of tobacco for each head brought before them.[29] The unpopulated condition of the colony had had the customary effect upon education. Schools of any advancement, with the notable exception of William and Mary, were still a thing of the future. The Bishop of London in 1723 had sent out to his forty clergymen a questionnaire regarding this subject, and with three reservations in favor of small charity institutions, he was told that no schools existed.

The question, Is there any parish library? met with a like response.[30] Elsewhere newspapers were coming into vogue. Boston had had one since 1704. Ben Franklin's brother had ventured another in 1719, and in 1725, a third was published in New York.[31] But Virginians were slow to adopt the fashion. The initiative had to be taken ten years later by an outsider, one William Parks, of Maryland. Berkeley's prayer against free schools and printing had apparently not fallen upon deaf ears.

The planter, rather, was content with his horses and the social graces of his century — conversation, dancing, and the theater. The extant colonial Virginia records are in no sense complete; yet the instance has been noted that in Accomac, on the eastern shore, a play called *Ye Beare and Ye Cubb* was performed as early as 1675 — seventy-five years before there is any evidence of dramatic entertainment in New York. A protest against this violent innovation was promptly registered in the county court, to be sure. The judges ordered the entire performance to be staged in costume before them. But they enjoyed it immensely, and the accuser paid the costs.[32]

In 1716, Williamsburg had acquired the first playhouse in America. One William Livingston, a merchant of the town, had for some time conducted a dancing-school in New Kent County. Two of his pupils, Charles and Mary

Stagg, developed a remarkable histrionic talent, and Livingston agreed to build a theater, with this couple as actors. He also provided scenery and music out of England 'for the enacting of comedies and tragedies.' [33] This fine custom survived throughout Byrd's lifetime. In 1736, Mrs. Stagg, as shall be seen, was still an active figure in the colonial capital, staging plays and assemblies that on General Court days in the spring and fall attracted a gay concourse of Virginia's most exclusive society. Culture, it seems, could never quite die out after the college was founded, for one of the clauses in William and Mary's charter called for a yearly contribution of Latin verses to the Governor.

At times the executive well deserved the lines that were written in his honor. What Virginian of the year 1726 could forget, for example, the gallant 'ultra-montaine' expedition Spotswood had made some ten years before — how he had pushed back into the wilderness a distance of four hundred and thirty-six miles; how he had used horseshoes for the first time and, to commemorate the occasion, founded among his companions the order of the Knights of the Golden Horseshoe! The scholars of William and Mary did not forget it — not immediately, at any rate. The conclusion of the translated Latin poem they presented the intrepid Scotchman upon his return serves for ample testimony:

> After the hero pass'd the gentle flood,
> Through which directly went their mirey road,
> Regardless of his charge he pausing stood:
> He thought, and then resolved without delay,
> Homewards to make his retrogressive way,

Having for George his king possession took,
And cut his name in ultra montaine rock.
Obeying then the dictates of his mind
He straight returned and left this scene behind;
Where he, like Hercules in former days,
Had made two mountains pillars of his praise.[34]

To this colony of mingled backwardness and charm, of studied aloofness and slave-swelled pomposity, Byrd brought his family in the summer of 1726. The change, though he rarely complained about it, must have oppressed him bitterly — as the differences between a highly urban and a sterile environment would have preyed upon any cultured man of his century. He had always been a person who could make the most of genuine adversity, or bear with a good-natured tolerance the petty reverses of the hour. The day was fast coming when this virtue would be sorely tried. Byrd doubtless foresaw it vaguely. But then there was London once more. After a time his debts would be wiped out, his pilgrimage to the new world over.

VIII

KING'S COMMISSIONER

Byrd was fifty-four years old, but he leaped across the table in front of him and seized Fitzwilliam's arm in time to prevent the probably fatal blow from descending. In his haste he, of course, overturned this piece of furniture, and one of the Carolina commissioners, who had rushed in, fell under it 'to the great hazard of his gouty limbs.'

I

BYRD's first few months in Virginia were crowded with activity. There were long-neglected business affairs to be straightened out. The condition of his slaves demanded attention. Overseers' accounts called for minute inspection. It was imperative, now, that his entire interests be rendered compatible with sound economics. For six years their management had been left to others, and he had not prospered. It was the price he had had to pay for the delights of London. But there were numberless compensations that justified this expense. He did not complain.

How pleasant a thing it was, for example, to correspond intimately with the third Lord Boyle, now just become of age and returned from his grand tour. What vivid pictures this young gentleman drew of the gay French Court of Louis XV! He described it, Byrd exclaimed, 'with so much life and propriety that I fancied the objects themselves present before my eyes!' [1] As Byrd sat at his dinner-table chatting with his daughters and wife, he recalled his own youth and gossiped merrily about the French. What a happy people they were, singing on short commons and dancing in wooden shoes, 'either of which,' he would add, 'made a true Briton very low-spirited. Most nationalities are very awkward when they are gay, but the French seem so only when melancholy.'[2]

Then there was Lady Sandwich, he remembered (intimate with King Louis himself), whose husband had invented the 'half a dinner' named after him. How was it a certain Cardinal had characterized her? She had, he had solemnly declared, 'la figure, et l'esprit le plus males qui j'aie connus a aucune femme.'[3] Especially la figure! How simply and well the churchman had hit her off. Byrd would then become serious and discourse upon the grand tour more gravely. Taken in general, it was a doubtful blessing. 'Most young fellows who go abroad,' he pronounced himself, 'improve in little besides confidence. This helps them to discover their whole stock of vice and folly, which bashfulness concealed in them before.'[4] The world certainly did not seem to him to be on the moral upgrade, when one compared the present younger generation with his own and Justice Lynde's.

To members of the Byrd household, news from Boyle was invariably an event. With it there would come a momentary living again in the world they had perforce forsaken. Letters, to Byrd himself, constituted his most vital and intimate tie with the past. They meant that he was still remembered by those whom he most admired. They served him as a sort of newspaper, keeping him informed as to what was happening in London and Paris — the faraway centers of things. He read them over and over. For days together their contents provided the important topic of conversation. Without these infrequent tidings from Europe, it was so easy to become lost in the world, the

WILLIAM BYRD OF WESTOVER
From a portrait painted about 1736
Only the head is original

victim of a sort of premature burial above ground, cut off, it seemed, from the living. For consolation, when his correspondents were slow in replying, Byrd turned countless times to the past and found a true though vicarious delight in literature. But there were always occasions when his spirit rebelled at this anæmic substitution of a printed page for the reality. A letter from a friend was able in some measure to transcend the disparity. Like its author, it was a living thing.

Byrd's delight in his young friend's description of the coronation of George II was well warranted. It was done in the very best manner.

The king burst into tears upon the news of his father's death [Boyle wrote], but later went to his royal consort's apartment to inform her of her new dignity. She received the news either with great joy or great sorrow, for she fell into an hysterick fitt, which excess of either passion will occasion. However, heaven preserved her for better days, and she came about five in the afternoon with her princely spouse to Leicester house.

Now the joyful scene appears, and it would need an abler painter than I am to describe it. Leicester Fields and all the streets near it were crowded with coaches. So many were the bonfires and illuminations that the town seemed all on fire. Bells, trumpets, and drums deafened the inhabitants; nothing but joy was seen; nothing but huzzas heard, and if you will allow a classical simile, it was like the rejoicing of the Trojans described in Virgil, when they thought the Grecians were run away.[5]

When Boyle went to congratulate the Queen, he adds: 'Her Majesty sent me away happy, by telling me with a smile that I was much grown since she had last seen me.' Virginia held nothing for Byrd that could rival in interest this young lord's brief note, brought him by some sea captain on his yearly voyage up the James.

It was on Byrd's fifty-third birthday, in 1727, that this new monarch authorized his appointment as one of the three Virginia commissioners who were to direct the surveying of the boundary line between that colony and North Carolina. The controversy regarding this important matter had long vexed both provinces. Its origin is traceable to the terms of the Carolina charters, the one of 1663 declaring that the colony should extend northward to the 36th degree of latitude, while a second, issued two years later, specified as its limits 'the north end of Currituck river or inlet upon a straight westerly line to Weyanoke Creek, which lies within the degrees of 36 and 30 minutes.' [6]

By the terms of the second charter, a strip of land approximately thirty miles wide was added to Carolina. But settlers holding property grants from the Virginia government (which, until 1701, seems to have ignored entirely the more recent claims of her neighbor) had meanwhile moved into the disputed area. The question of jurisdiction was clearly not determined, and according to Byrd's friend, Professor Hugh Jones, of William and Mary College, at least one element of the population made the most of this uncertainty. The tract in dispute constituted a sort of 'American mint,' he affirmed, 'whither wicked and profligate persons retire, being out of the certain jurisdiction of either government, where they may pursue any immoral or vicious practices without censure and with impunity.' [7]

To the Reverend Jones, firmly ecclesiastic, the resolution of the whole matter was simple. Why not grant the controverted territory to a 'Bishop of Virginia and North

Carolina?' he asks. It would hasten the fulfillment of one of his ferventest prayers:

> God bless the Church, and George its defender,
> Convert the Fanaticks, and baulk the Pretender.[8]

But if the secular arm insists upon its rights, then employ the mathematics professor of the college to compute the area jointly claimed and give to each colony its half.

Neither of these recommendations seems to have met with the approval it doubtless deserved. And after forty-seven years of intermittent complaints on the part of both governments (during which time one actually begun joint survey had ended unsuccessfully because of certain obstructionary tactics on the part of the North Carolina commissioners), the matter had reached such a stage as to demand some permanent determination.[9] To this end His Majesty, in the event of another difference between the representatives of the two provinces, wisely empowered Byrd and his associates, Richard Fitzwilliam and William Dandridge, to finish the work alone.[10]

The Virginians, thus armed with King George's commission, planned the survey in an elaborate manner. Lest their neighbors should happen to be taken by surprise, Byrd deemed it proper to acquaint them with the exact nature of their preparations

that so you gentlemen, who are appointed in this same station, may, if you please, do the same honor to your government. We shall have a tent with us and a marquee for the convenience of ourselves and our servants. We shall be provided with as much wine and rum as will enable us and our men to drink every night to the success of the following day, and because we understand that there are many Gentiles on your frontier who never had an opportunity of being baptized, we shall have a chaplain to make them Christians. For this purpose we intend to rest in our camp every Sunday that there may be leisure for so good a work. And whoever of your province shall be desirous of novelty may report on Sundays to our tent and hear a sermon. Of this you may please give notice, that the charitable intentions of the government may meet with the happier success.[11]

After considerable preliminary correspondence, the joint commissioners met at Currituck Inlet on March 5, 1728. Readings gave this place a latitude of 36° 31'. Naturally enough, the work began with a dispute as to the points from which the line should start. Byrd's party contended that it should be the spit of sand on the north shore of the inlet. The Carolinians insisted upon a stretch of high ground two hundred yards beyond. The gentlemen produced their respective commissions.

And to the end that our service herein may not be disappointed [Byrd read his own orders from the King aloud] through the refusal or delay of the Commissioners for North Carolina to act in conjunction with you, we do hereby give and grant unto you full power and authority to cause the said line to be run and marked out, any opposition of the said Commissioners of North Carolina notwithstanding.[12]

The Carolinians were non-plussed; for their own orders, as one may well surmise, contained no such imperious clause. It was much 'too lordly and positive,' obviously giving the opposition the whip hand. But their protests were met by the bluff reply that the previous boundary commission had been thwarted by just such vacillation and quibblings as were at that moment in evidence.

Yet the Virginians, exemplifying a rare magnanimity,

finally conceded the starting-point, and a temporary outward harmony ensued. A cedar post was then erected and
from it a due course westward was taken. Across rivers
and islands, over creeks and marshes, through wild and
settled areas, this party (composed jointly of forty laborers, seven commissioners, four surveyors, and a chaplain)
proceeded until, on March 12, they were close to the
hitherto unexplored Dismal Swamp.

For the first time they realized that their work was soon
to become serious. Day began ominously. Byrd was
hardly awake before complaint reached him that some
Indians had stolen his men's meat while they slept. 'This
provoked me,' he confessed, 'to treat them a la dragoon,
that is to swear at them furiously; and by the good grace of
my oaths I might have passed for a trooper in His Majesty's guards.' [13] Rain the night before and the consequent
necessity of drying bedclothes and foraging prevented their
starting out before twelve o'clock.

The commissioners sensed the futility of attempting to
accomplish very much the remainder of the afternoon and
proceeded to take their work lightly. Encountering a propitious location, they quit for the day and were soon making merry around a cheerful bowl. 'In the gaiety of their
hearts,' Byrd tells us, 'they invited a tallow-faced wench
who had sprained her wrist to drink with them; and when
they had raised her in good humor, they examined all her
hidden charms and played a great many similar pranks.' [14]
So their amusements continued, far into the evening, 'the
poor damsel disabled from making any resistance by the
lameness of her hand.' Byrd retired early, but about midnight one of the Carolinians grew envious of his neighbor's

delights and ventured a visit to their camp. 'And his curiousity was so very clamorous,' Byrd declared, 'that it waked me, for which I wished his nose as flat as any of his procivorous countrymen.'

Two days later the party reached the Dismal. Byrd, who of course as a commissioner had no intentions of following the surveyors through the swamp, decided that they needed a final brief haranguing. 'Gentlemen,' he began, 'we are at last arrived at this dreadful place, which until now has been thought impassable. But I make no doubt you will convince everybody that there is no difficulty which may not be conquered by spirit and constancy. I protest to you the only reason I don't share in your fatigue is the fear of adding to your burdens (which are but too heavy already) while I am sure I can add nothing to your resolution. I shall say no more but only pray the Almighty to prosper your undertaking and grant we may meet on the other side in perfect health and safety.' Yet he could not but observe that 'the men took this speech very kindly, and answered it in the most cheerful manner with three huzzas.' [15]

The commissioners, it should certainly be said, were as solicitous about their men as one could reasonably ask. Only twelve of the entire company were actually employed with the surveyors in making their route through the Swamp itself. Byrd and the others found their way around, keeping always near the edge and firing occasional volleys which, if heard, would be answered by the laborers within. One week after his speech, on March 22, news came that their detachment was safely out again. It had required this time to traverse a distance of fifteen miles.[16]

But the work was becoming tedious. Dandridge, one of the commissioners, was ill. Byrd treated him as ably as he might with ipecac. For Fitzwilliam, his other associate, he had never entertained a very complimentary opinion. This gentleman (Firebrand, he called him) sided with the Carolinians in whatever disputes arose. If it happened to be a difference between the surveyors of the two colonies, Fitzwilliam was uniformly partial to the opposition. It was little short of treason.

On the evening of March 26, Byrd says that he took a solitary walk, 'that I might have leisure to think on my absent friends, whom I now grew impatient to see.' [17] But he could not avoid noting how intimate were Fitzwilliam and the North Carolina surveyor. The latter, he says, 'stuck as close to his patron as the itch does to the fingers of many of his country folk.'

Time continued to drag heavily. The twenty-eighth came. It was Byrd's birthday. That evening he again went for a walk alone and, remembering his age, 'adored the goodness of heaven for having indulged me with so much health and very uncommon happiness in the course of fifty-four years in which my sins have been many and my sufferings few, my opportunities great, but my improvements small.' [18]

Eight days later the commissioners decided to suspend further work on the survey until autumn. It was April. Snakes were becoming dangerous, and the men appeared exhausted from their six weeks in the wilderness. They had carried the line as far west as the Meharrin River, a distance of seventy-three miles,[19] and the most trying phase of their labors, the Dismal, was over.

On the twentieth of September they resumed their task. Soon the party reached Roanoke River, whose rich bottoms so impressed Byrd that he later purchased some twenty thousand acres there and, after Governor Eden, of Carolina, named the property the Land of Eden. Things could hardly be regarded as progressing smoothly. Dandridge and Fitzwilliam no longer spoke to each other, and Byrd's civilities to the latter were of the most forced sort. But through Fitzwilliam's consorting constantly with the Carolinians, an open breach was for a while avoided.

Matters came to a head on the fifth of October. One of the Carolina commissioners rode up to Byrd and told him that his colleagues would like to speak with him. 'I desired them,' said Byrd, 'if they had anything to communicate, they would please come forward.' For a time nothing happened. But finally another member of their commission did ride up and inform Byrd that their government had ordered them to run the line but thirty or forty miles above the Roanoke, that they had now carried it nearly fifty, and intended to go no farther.[20]

'I let them know,' he wrote, 'that it was a little unkind that they had not been so gracious as to acquaint us with their intentions before; that it would have been neighborly to have informed us ere we set out how far they intended to go, that we might also have received the commands of our government in the matter; but since they had failed in that civility we would go on without them; that it was a great misfortune to lose their company; but that it would be a much greater one to lose the effect of our expedition by doing the business by halves.'[21]

Each side thereupon drew up elaborate written arguments, justifying its actions. The North Carolina commissioners set forth that the important question of the long controversy (whether Nottaway River or Wicocon Creek corresponded to the mythical Weyanoke) had been settled in their favor, as indeed it had, and the most difficult labor of the survey already performed. They added that the region of uninhabited lands had been reached, and that when necessary the line could be extended through this section by two or three surveyors, instead of the large and expensive party then employed. To this Byrd replied characteristically that his instructions were to finish the line, that settlers would in a few years be pushing forward into the fertile and unsurveyed lands beyond the Roanoke, and that 'expense should not be taken into account when the public interest was at stake.' [22]

Now Byrd had said all these things orally to the Carolinians when the dispute first came up. That night after supper he rehearsed the scene before his colleagues. He desired that Fitzwilliam in particular should know his mind on the subject. But the discussion was no sooner begun before Fitzwilliam demanded that Byrd produce his commission and show the clause upon which he based his claim to the right of continuing the survey without his neighbors' coöperation.

'I gave him to understand,' declared Byrd, 'that since the commissioners were the same who acted before, all of whom had heard the document read, I had not thought it necessary to cram my portmanteau with it a second time.' [23]

'I'll make a minute of this,' shouted Fitzwilliam, and so wrote to the effect that having asked for a sight of Mr.

Byrd's commission, he was denied it, upon the 'pretense' that Mr. Byrd had it not with him.

Byrd objected to the word 'pretense,' and Fitzwilliam was compelled to change it. The latter then insisted with some extravagance that the Virginia Governor had told him it would suffice to run the line some thirty or forty miles beyond Roanoke River.

'Ha ha!' roared Dandridge unceremoniously, lugging out his pencil. 'By God, since you're for minutes, I'll make a minute of that.'

This was too much. Without another word Fitzwilliam snatched off the leg of a table 'big enough to knock down an ox,' and prepared to demolish his antagonist. Byrd was fifty-four years old, but he leaped across the table in front of him and seized Fitzwilliam's arm in time to prevent the probably fatal blow from descending. In his haste, he of course overturned this piece of furniture, and one of the Carolina commissioners, who had rushed in, fell under it 'to the great hazard of his gouty limbs.' [24]

'As soon as Dandridge came to know the favor Fitzwilliam intended him,' Byrd continues, 'he saluted him with the title he had a good right to, namely, a son of a whore, telling him that if they had been alone he durst as well be damned as lift that club against him. To this the other replied with as much vigor that he might remember, if he pleased, that he had now lifted a club at him.' [25]

Like most public quarrels, this one ended without bloodshed. But Byrd was apprehensive lest a duel should soon follow, 'because in a court of honor,' he explains, 'the shaking of a cudgel at a gentleman is adjudged the same affront as striking him with it.' When Fitzwilliam came up the

following afternoon, therefore, and seemed sincerely disposed to friendliness, Byrd took advantage of the offer and
reconciled him and Dandridge to such an extent that 'at
last I joined their hands and made them kiss one another.'[26]

This act seemingly opened the way for a common settling
of differences between the two commissions. They proceeded to attribute their previous quarrel to disagreements
in the realm of principle, drank to each other's very good
health, and parted with enthusiastic professions of friendship — 'just as some men and their wives,' Byrd could not
but think, 'who, after living together all their time in per-
petual discord and uneasiness, will yet be very amiable at
the point of death, when they are sure they will part forever.' [27] He was also constrained to add that 'a general joy
discovered itself through all our camp when these gentlemen turned their backs upon us.'

Byrd's party pushed the line some seventy-five miles
farther on before they reached the Appalachian foothills,
and, because of the advanced season, relinquished their
work. In all the survey had extended a distance of two
hundred and forty-one miles. This proved to be sufficient
during Byrd's lifetime, but a few years thereafter another
joint commission ran it an additional ninety miles westward.

2

It seems that the journal Byrd kept of this expedition —
later expanded into his *History of the Dividing Line* — was
inspired by motives primarily mercenary. He wanted to
ensure adequate payment both for himself and his men,
and wisely concluded that this end could best be accom-

plished through sending to the sedate Lords of Trade a record of their difficulties. Upon his return to Westover, he
promptly dispatched this thirty-two-page document to
England, accompanying it with a letter emphasizing the
hardships his men had labored under. The Lords of Trade
acknowledged the receipt of both in the fall of 1729,[28] and
sanctioned an appropriation of one thousand pounds to
meet all expenses. Byrd's commissioner's share amounted
to one hundred and forty-two pounds.

He was really in need of this sum and more, for in December, 1728, he had purchased that twenty thousand
acres near the fertile Roanoke River bottoms known as the
Land of Eden. By his own statement it appears that the
North Carolina government had no means of paying its
dividing-line commissioners other than by granting them
certain of the tracts they had recently surveyed.[29] Byrd
bought this particular property from one of the more im-
pecunious of these gentlemen for two hundred pounds. He
had a difficult time keeping it. A few months after his
patent was signed, the North Carolina proprietors sold all
their rights to the Crown, and the colony came under royal
control. The King's representative, Governor Johnson,
was informed that Byrd had not acquired his title prior to
His Majesty's purchase. It was not until 1736, and only
after what seemed unbearable exactions upon his patience
that Byrd's ownership at last received his sovereign's bene-
diction.

Meanwhile, Byrd had conceived a highly original plan in
regard to the Dismal Swamp. It appeared to him a la-
mentable waste that this vast expanse of fertile territory
(thirty by ten miles according to his estimate) should be of

no service. Why not drain it? Such a venture would give inland Carolina a water outlet. It would greatly facilitate trade. The soil reclaimed would be the most suitable in the world for the then highly desired hemp. And from a standpoint of health, the attendant advantages were quite too obvious to mention.[30] Byrd submitted his proposal to Colonel Bladen in London, requesting that he interest some wealthy Englishmen in the enterprise.[31] He wanted to form a stock company with a capital of four thousand pounds. One half the amount would be subscribed in Virginia, the remainder in London, 'that the project may have friends on both sides of the water.' Within ten years, he enthusiastically asserted, the investment should pay ten for one.[32]

Byrd's plans took cognizance of the most obscure details. All actual work was, of course, to be done by slaves. Ten of them, seasoned, of both sexes would be purchased the first year, 'that their breed may supply the loss from death.' As far as possible, the project was to carry on itself. These negroes, their number augmented by small yearly purchases and, naturally, by birth, would do all the labor and raise their own food. Thus the owners would have a colony of some three hundred blacks, in addition to an expanse of valuable drained property, by the time the ten years had expired.[33]

But this ably thought-out if somewhat nebulous plan came to grief on the shoals of British materialism. The collapse of the South Sea bubble a decade before had made the investors of England wary of one thousand per cent dividends in the new world. That this particular proposition appeared a good one, they admitted. But capital was no longer adventurous. Byrd finally abandoned the idea. Yet an interest in it was revived once more, nineteen years after his death, and no less a notable than young George Washington was the gentleman whom those concerned engaged to be their surveyor.

IX

MAN OF LETTERS

'But in justice to our Carolina friends,' he remarked with indulgence, 'they stuck with us as long as our liquor lasted and were so kind as to drink our good journey to the mountains in the last bottle we had left.'

I

THE *History of the Dividing Line* in its present form represents an elaboration of the rough diary Byrd made during the surveying expedition and sent to the Lords of Trade to ensure adequate compensation for his work. It is probable that before completing the final manuscript he had written the recently discovered *Secret History* [1] and received several compliments upon its merits.

But this encouragement did not turn his head. He was determined that before any wide circle of English friends should be allowed to read his literary efforts, he would work them over to his entire satisfaction. An old London friend, Peter Collinson, upon learning that he was rewriting his earlier draft, entreated him for a sight of the new one. Byrd would not consent.

I must own it goes against me to deny you such a trifle [he wrote], but I have one infirmity — never to venture anything unfinished out of my hands. The bashful bears hide their cubs until they have licked them into shape, nor am I too proud to follow the example of those modest animals. If Solomon sends lazy people to the ants to learn industry, all authors should not be ashamed to go to the bears, to be instructed never to produce any offspring of theirs until they have brought it into shape fit to be seen. [2]

That Byrd really did think of publishing the *History* ultimately appears from a request he made of this same gentleman the following year. He explained that he would finish his writing the coming winter, and that, as he intended to describe some of Virginia's wild animals, he would appreciate Collinson's making arrangements for some cuts.[3] But during his lifetime the volume never came out.

One doubts that he ever seriously attempted publication, for here, too, the shadow of the bad bargain he had made years before protracted itself. He had even found it necessary — and we cannot know with what humiliation — to confess his sad plight to friends in England. He begged them to use their influence in extracting him 'from the gripe of an usurer.' His complaints became chronic, almost annoying, the importunities of an old man who cried out because his burdens were too heavy to be borne. And compared to this misery the halo of authorship had waned into a glimmer of no moment.

2

Byrd very likely dictated the *History of the Dividing Line* to his librarian and secretary, Mr. Proctor. The unhurried manner in which he wrote suggests his philosophy of authorship. One's literary output should reflect, he believed, the essence of a lifetime of observation. It should clarify itself as a by-product of one's leisure hours, written chiefly for the delight of friends. And, in truth, the *History* does disclose the rich associations that years of sincere delight in books had brought him. The outward form of a work was of small importance. He chose the journal because it allowed him most freedom in expressing his own individuality.

As the comic spirit has rarely if ever flourished as it did within the period of Byrd's youth, it is not strange to find that he was himself saturated with it. The explanation is obvious. Byrd was by nature and inheritance essentially moral. His ethical standards and social principles were eminently definite. Like Addison and Steele and the little Queen Anne's man who had entertained his daughter, he was acutely aware of what rational behavior on all occasions ought to comprise.

It was this highly positive sense of an elevated criterion of conduct, this incisive awareness of how things ought to be, that made of Byrd primarily a humorist. For humor is the result of an indulgent appreciation of the disparity between the ideal and the actual, between the profession and the practice. To Byrd, by way of example, the only standard of living worthy of acceptance was the aristocratic; and those who, like the North Carolinians, could not achieve it (especially those who tried but failed) he made the butt of his jests.

And there were the New-Englanders, overly mercenary, mean traders who drove hard bargains without ceremony; or the grossly religious Quakers. He disliked both, because to the Virginian of his time it was bad form to take either Commerce or the Deity with unbecoming seriousness. Consider the grave probability one risked of making one's self inconsistent or absurd! The saints of New England, of such vehemently professed godliness, were the very rascals who sold their rotten rum up and down the coast and considered it a rare accomplishment to evade the payment of fees due His Majesty under the Navigation Laws.

And with the Quakers, it was necessary, to document one's contempt for them, only to go back a few decades to the private life of Mr. William Penn himself. 'This ingenious person,' we should not forget, 'had not been bred a Quaker, but in his earlier days had been a man of pleasure about the town. He had a beautiful form and very taking address which made him successful with the ladies and particularly with a mistress of the Duke of Monmouth. By this gentlewoman he had a daughter who had beauty enough to raise her to be a duchess, and continued to be a toast full thirty years. But this amour had like to have brought our fine gentleman in danger of a duel, had he not discreetly sheltered himself under this Peaceable Persuasion.' [4]

This pronounced class consciousness in Byrd is plainly revealed by comparing the *Secret History* with the *History of the Dividing Line*. The former work, with its constant use of fictitious names,[5] Byrd doubtless wrote first for the entertainment of his most intimate acquaintance. In it he said exactly what he thought of Virginians and Carolinians alike. The *Secret History* is for this reason a much more reliable account of the facts of the expedition.

When Byrd considered publication, however, his prudence did not desert him. He realized at once that the tacit thesis of his work (that Virginia was the most admirable, civilized, and aristocratic of the colonies) would suffer decidedly if he obtruded into the narrative any reference to the petty dispute which had occurred during the survey between himself and Fitzwilliam. The *History of the Dividing*

Line, in print, was to picture Virginians in a wholly admirable light.

But how could such a purpose be successful if the world were informed that on six different occasions members of the Virginia party had offered violence to women?[6] And what would the average reader think of Byrd's own ability at discipline if, disapproving of such outrages, he failed in his efforts to stop them? These facts, plainly, were not for vulgar ears. Certain favored fellow Virginians or a few aristocratic London friends might in a *Secret History* enjoy an account of such details well enough. But not the average reader. In the version intended for the average reader they were accordingly omitted.

Byrd's artistic sense was also active. Along with the incidents of violence, he deleted from the manuscript as intended for publication five speeches which he had delivered to his men. As his remarks were in large measure occasional and of little importance, he realized their relative unsuitableness in a permanent history. The same reason probably accounts for his omission of three letters exchanged by the rival commissions before their first meeting.

An explanation of the most singular divergence between the two works (the fact that the *Secret History* contains only one unfavorable comment on North Carolinians while the *History* itself abounds in such references) has already been suggested. Byrd knew that the readiest way in which to exalt his own colony was by disparaging every other. He concentrated upon his neighbors to the south. Yet Maryland, New York, and New England in general, as has been seen, did not escape unmentioned.

Thus Byrd's best-known literary work, an outgrowth of a practical desire to ensure payment for himself and his men, had its basis in a purpose oddly resembling propaganda. But it had something else which distinguished it altogether from typically evangelistic writing and which made it a work of admitted literary art. Byrd was a man of wide and varied experience, of keen insight and incisive wit. He was this much more truly than he was a propagandist. It was inescapable, in consequence, that his implied purpose should in the course of his writing remain such in vague outline only. It was equally inescapable that his absorbing accounts of what he observed in the backwoods, colored though they be by his imagination and prejudices, should emerge the major items of interest to readers. The *History* as a final literary product stands as an admirable commentary upon the fact that in the work of the truly gifted artist a special purpose will always, if the writer gives freedom to his personality, become subordinate to the portrayal of life itself.

3

In the *History of the Dividing Line*, Byrd's prejudices are apparent from the start. The entire Atlantic seaboard, he would have us know, 'went at first under the general name of Virginia,' and all other colonies formed thereafter represent a sort of lopping-off of limbs from the mother torso.

Virginia was named for the virgin queen Elizabeth, whom one remembers most pleasantly because of her first experience 'with that bewitching vegetable, tobacco.' Sir

Walter, upon his return from the colony, 'thought he could do no less than make a present of some of the brightest of this commodity to his royal mistress, for her own smoking. The Queen graciously accepted of it, but finding her stomach sicken after two or three whiffs, it was presently whispered by the Earl of Leicester's faction that Raleigh had certainly poisoned her. But Her Majesty, soon recovering her disorder, obliged the Countess of Nottingham and all her maids to smoke a whole pipe out amongst them.' [7]

But the evil days were close at hand. New England was pared off from Virginia in 1620. New York soon followed. Next came Pennsylvania, and then, most lamentably of all, Maryland. The *History* continues its survey of the past to the culmination of the dividing-line controversy, and for all its readability and good humor appears about as reliable as the more serious works of Byrd's contemporaries.

His character sketches are rarely dull. He had no sooner recorded setting up the cedar post that marked the line's point of departure than he felt compelled to digress, by way of paying his respects to a mariner who lived near by.

This man [he notes] modestly called himself a hermit, though he forfeited that name by suffering a wanton female to cohabit with him.

His habitation was a bower, covered with bark after the Indian fashion which in that mild situation protected him pretty well from the weather. Like the ravens, he neither plowed or sowed but subsisted chiefly upon oysters which his handmaid made a shift to gather from the adjacent rocks. Sometimes, too, for change of diet he sent her to drive up the neighbor's cows to moisten their mouths with a little milk. But as for raiment, he depended mostly upon his length of beard, and she upon her length of hair, part of which she brought decently forward, and the rest dangled behind quite down to the rump, like one of Herodotus's east Indian pigmies.

Thus did these wretches live in a dirty state of nature and were mere Adamites, innocence only excepted.[8]

The members of Byrd's party presented a queer appearance indeed. When they came into a neighborhood, people invariably flocked about them. 'The men left their beloved chimney corners, the good women their spinning wheels, and some, of more curiosity than ordinary, rose out of their sick beds to come and stare at us.' Those spectators who were more favorably impressed regarded them as 'a troup of knight errants' running great risks for the public weal. Others usually took them for criminals, 'condemned to this dirty work for offenses against the state.'

The *History*, as has already been seen, is notorious for its author's amusing disesteem of everything relating to North Carolina. Chronologically, Byrd was no pioneer in this respect. One remembers, of course, Spotswood's contempt for the Carolina Assembly. The Reverend Hugh Jones had commented upon his neighbors almost as unfavorably in 1724.

That colony is vastly inferior to Virginia. Its trade is smaller and its inhabitants thinner. As for churches, there are but very few, and I know of but one minister in the whole government. He (for what reason I know not) had no great faculty for influencing the people and is lately removed hence, so that much religion cannot be expected among a collection of such people as fly thither from other places of safety and livelihood.[9]

Like Byrd, this churchman rested his faith only in his fellow colonists.

If New England be called the receptacle of dissenters and an Amsterdam of religion, Pennsylvania the nursery of Quakers, Maryland the retirement of Roman Catholics, North Carolina the refuge of runaways, and South Carolina the delight of buccaneers and pirates — Virginia may be justly esteemed the happy retreat of brave Britons and true churchmen.[10]

And this, one may be sure, represents no mere rhetorical flourish, but is precisely the way the residents of the Old Dominion felt about the matter.

Byrd disliked his North Carolina neighbors primarily for their indolence. 'We observed very few cornfields in that country,' he tells us, 'and those very small, which seemed the stranger to us because we could see no other tokens of husbandry or improvement.' But upon further inquiry he was given to understand that these people only made corn for themselves and not for their stocks, 'which know very well how to get their own living.'

Both cattle and hogs rambled in the neighboring marshes and swamps, where they maintained themselves the whole winter long and were not fetched home till the spring. 'Thus these indolent wretches during one half of the year lose the advantage of the milk of their cattle, as well as their dung, and many of the poor creatures by this ill management perish in the mire into the bargain. Some who pique themselves more upon industry than their neighbors will now and then, out of compliment to their cattle, cut down a tree whose limbs are loaded with moss.' The trouble of climbing the tree in order to gather this provender would, of course, be too great. 'The shortest way (which in this country is always counted the best) is to fell it, just like the lazy Indians, who do the same by such trees as bear fruit and so make one harvest for all.' By this bad husbandry, milk was so scarce in the winter season 'that were a big-bellied woman to long for it, she would lose her longing. And in truth I believe this is often the case and at the same time a very good reason why so many people in this province are marked with a custard complexion.' [11]

The Carolinians were great pork eaters, and certain maladies attending this monotonous diet often were known very treacherously 'to undermine the foundations of their noses.' Indeed, Byrd notes, 'this calamity is so common and familiar here that it ceases to be a scandal, and in the disputes that happen about beauty, the noses have in some company much ado to carry it.' The rumor even persisted that once, after three good pork years, a motion was contemplated in the Carolina House of Burgesses 'that a man with a nose should be incapable of holding any place of profit in the province.' And a law so unique could never have been introduced 'without some hopes of a majority.' It was a knowledge of the ill effects of eating swine's flesh in hot countries that made that questionable delicacy 'an abomination to the Jews, who lived much in the same latitude with Carolina.' [12]

'Surely,' Byrd elsewhere declares, 'there is no place in the world where the inhabitants live with less labor than in North Carolina. It approaches nearer to the description of Lubberland than any other, by the great felicity of the climate, the easiness of raising provisions, and the slothfulness of the people.' [13]

This censoriousness cropped out even in descriptions of the Dismal. The swamp itself was well named, if we may believe Byrd's lively chronicle. 'Not even a turkey-buzzard will venture to fly over it, no more than the Italian vultures will fly over the filthy lake Avernus, or the birds in the Holy Land over the salt sea, where Sodom and Gomorrah formerly stood.' But his men were laboring bravely in the very midst of this place. 'The best we could do for them,' he notes, 'was to give them a place in the litany.' The chaplain did his part well, 'rubbing us up with a seasonable sermon.' This, of course, 'was quite a new thing to our brethren of North Carolina, who live in a climate where no clergyman can breathe, any more than spiders in Ireland.' [14]

Byrd rehearsed the dispute over the survey's termination in the lordliest manner. He was a Virginian, acting upon His Majesty's expressed commission, and he meant to do the work thoroughly. 'But in justice to our Carolina friends,' he remarked with indulgence, 'they stuck by us as long as our liquor lasted and were so kind as to drink our good journey to the mountains in the last bottle we had left.' [15] 'Thereafter,' he added elsewhere, 'we had no other drink but what Adam drank in Paradise. Though to our comfort we found the water excellent, by the help of which we perceived our appetites to mend, our slumbers to sweeten, the stream of life to run cool and peaceably in our veins, and if ever we dreamed of women, they were kind.' [16]

But Byrd seems most to have enjoyed writing about Indians — a race that to a prospective European audience was a source of endless curiosity. One Sunday evening his party visited the Nottoway tribe. They were received in great state, amid much whooping, war dancing, and other shows of hospitality.

Quite characteristically, Byrd's appraising eye sought out the ladies of the community. 'And though their complexions be a little sad colored,' he notes, 'yet their shapes are very straight and well-proportioned. Their faces are seldom handsome, yet they have an air of innocence and bashfulness that with a little less dirt would not fail to make them desirable. Such charms might have had their full effect upon our men, who had been so long deprived of female conversation, but that the whole winter's soil was so crusted on the skins of those dark angels that it required a very strong appetite to approach them.'

Byrd could not but admire the practical genius of these women. 'The bear's oil with which they anoint their persons all over makes their skins soft and at the same time protects them from every species of vermin that use to be troublesome to other uncleanly people.'

His party was unluckily so large that the Indians could not well make them the compliment of bedfellows, according to their rules of hospitality. 'But a grave matron whispered one of the commissioners very civilly in the ear that if her daughter had been but one year older, she should have been at his devotion.' [17]

And Byrd could not avoid adding that upon the departure of his men 'our chaplain observed with concern that the ruffles of our fellow travellers were a little discolored with pochoon, wherewith, the good man had been told, those ladies used to improve their invisible charms.' [18]

From Byrd's account it appears that the project of

Indian education made possible by Boyle's charity was proving a futile investment. Many children of the natives his party visited were alumni of William and Mary College. They had especially been taught 'the principles of the Christian religion until they came to be men. Yet after they returned home,' he declares, 'instead of civilizing and converting the rest, they have immediately relapsed into barbarism themselves.' [19]

Byrd deplored this sad state of affairs, to be sure. But as a result of much deliberation upon the whole Indian question, he had, it seems, at last hit upon its only true solution. To his very judicious way of thinking there was 'but one way of converting these poor infidels and reclaiming them from barbarity, and that is charitably to intermarry with them, according to the modern policy of the most christian king in Canada and Louisiana.' [20]

If the English had been foresighted enough to do this when they first settled in America, 'the infidelity of the Indians had been worn out at this day, with their dark complexions, and the country had swarmed with people more than it does with insects.' It was certainly an unreasonable nicety, he goes on to say, that prevented these early colonists from entering into so good-natured an alliance. 'All nations of men have the same natural dignity, and we know that very bright talents may be lodged under a very dark skin.' The Indians by no means want understanding, and in figure they are tall and very well-proportioned.

'Even their copper colored complexion,' he declares, with an unwonted race confidence, 'would admit of blanching, if not in the first, at the farthest in the second generation. I may safely venture to say that the Indian women would have made altogether as honest wives for the first planters as the damsels they used to purchase from aboard the ships.' It thus seemed strange to him that any good Christian should have 'refused a wholesome straight bedfellow when he might have had so fair a portion of her as the merit of saving her soul.'

But the Indians' own religion seems to have interested Byrd extremely. He had employed a native named Bearskin to hunt for his party and took occasion one night to examine him concerning the faith of his fathers. 'He told us he believed there was one supreme god who had several subaltern deities under him and that this master god made the world a long time ago.' This god told the sun, the moon, and the stars their several businesses in the beginning, and with good looking after 'they have faithfully performed them ever since.' Bearskin thought that God had created many worlds before this, but that those worlds either grew old and ruinous or were destroyed because of the dishonesty of the inhabitants.

This god was very just and very good — ever well pleased with men who possess godlike qualities. He took good people into his safe protection, made them rich, 'filled their bellies plentifully, preserved them from sickness and from being surprised or overcome by their enemies. But all such as tell lies and cheat those they have dealings with, he never failed to punish with sickness, poverty, and hunger, and after all that, suffered them to be knocked on the head and scalped by those that fight against them.'

After death, he believed, both good and bad people

were conducted by a guard into a great road in which departed souls traveled together for some time. At a certain distance this road forked into two paths, the one extremely level and the other stony and mountainous. 'Here the good were parted from the bad by a flash of lightning, the first being hurried away to the right, the other to the left.' The right hand path led to a charming warm country, 'where the spring was everlasting and every month was May. And as the year is always in its youth, so the people and particularly the women, who seem bright as stars and never scold. In this happy climate there were deer, turkeys, elks, and buffalo innumerable, perpetually fat and gentle. The soil brought forth corn spontaneously, without the curse of labor, and so very wholesome that none who had the happiness to eat of it were ever sick, or grow old, or dy.'

Near the entrance into this blessed land sat a venerable man on a richly woven mat. He examined strictly all those who were brought before him, and if they had behaved well, the guards were ordered to open the crystal gate and let them enter into the land of delights.

The left path was very rugged and uneven, leading to a dark and barren country where it was always winter. The ground was covered the whole year round with snow, and nothing was to be seen upon the trees but icicles. All the people were hungry, yet had not a morsel of anything to eat except a bitter kind of potato 'that gave them the dry-grypes and filled their whole body with loathsome ulcers. Here all the women were old and ugly, having claws like a panther with which they flew upon the men who slighted their passion. For it seemed these haggard old furies were intolerantly fond and expected a vast deal of cherishing. They talked much and exceedingly shrill, giving exquisite pain to the drum of the ear which in that place of torment was so tender that every sharp note wounded it to the quick.'

At the end of the path sat a dreadful old woman on a monstrous toadstool. Her head was covered with rattle-snakes instead of tresses. 'This hag pronounced sentence of woe upon all the miserable wretches who held up their hands at her tribunal. After this, they were delivered over to huge turkey-buzzards, like harpies, that flew away with them to the place above mentioned. And here, after they had been tormented a certain number of years (according to their several degrees of guilt), they were again driven back into this world to try if they would mend their manners and merit a place the next time in the regions of bliss. This was the substance of Bearskin's religion, and,' Byrd indulgently observed, 'was as much to the purpose as could be expected from a mere state of nature, without one glimpse of revelation or philosophy.' [21]

Yet Bearskin had a rare sense of humor and was possibly the favorite acquaintance Byrd made on the entire trip. Like Lear, he once asked the cause of thunder of a philosopher in the party. 'The man told him merrily,' Byrd recounts, 'that the god of the English people was firing his great guns upon the god of the Indians, which made all the roaring in the clouds, and that the lightning was only the flash of those guns. The Indian replied very gravely that he believed that might be the case indeed and that the rain which followed upon the thunder was occasioned by the Indian god being so scared he could not hold his water.' [22]

As the work progressed, Byrd devoted considerable attention to the flora and fauna he encountered. Travel books given over to description of strange animals and miraculous incidents comprised his favorite reading. With what startled curiosity he perused his 'voyages' to Jamaica, Newfoundland, far away India or China — any place that savored of the unknown! Nothing was too incredible, no natural history too grossly unnatural. His age was just emerging into a full consciousness of the infinitely varied life the three previous centuries had discovered. Byrd was convinced that the indigenous specimens he saw should be noted. And he seems to have taken the accounts of others at their face value, never suspecting the part that imagination very likely played in completing their pictures.

Animal habits, in particular, come in for elaborate disquisitions. There was the 'Canterbury tale' of a settler who wandered into the Dismal and lost himself. He would very likely have famished in this quagmire had he not turned his ingenuity to very good account. 'He took a fat louse out of his collar and exposed it to the open day on a piece of white paper.' And the 'poor insect, having no eyelids, turned himself about 'till he found the darkest part of the heavens, and so made the best of his way towards the north.' And thus was the wanderer delivered.

The diligence of his own men in this swamp reminded Byrd of the curiously persistent Norway mice. They 'march in mighty armies,' he recounts, 'destroying all the fruits of the earth as they go along. But something peculiar to these obstinate little animals is that nothing stops them in their mad career, and if a house happen to stand in the way, disdaining to go an inch around, they crawl up one side of it and down the other. Or if they meet with any river, they are so determined that they swim directly over it without varying one point from their course for the sake of any safety or convenience.' [23] And so, he very generously implies, did his own surveyors proceed through the Dismal.

The fierceness of wildcats engaged him extremely, in particular their habit, when disabled, 'of tearing their flesh for very madness.' But 'the *false belly* of the female opossum' was truly nature's rarest performance. Into this unique orifice the animal's young retreat in time of danger, and, queerest of all, 'the female can draw the slit which is the inlet to this pouch so close that you must look narrowly to find it, especially if she happen to be a virgin.'

Then, of course, there was the inevitable polecat. Byrd described it in most lavish detail — from the surpassing sweetness of its roasted flesh to the distinctive potency of its major weapon of defense. For even as some brutes have horns and hoofs, and others claws, teeth, and tusks for their protection, and as still others are endowed only with their tongues, 'so the poor polecat's safety lies altogether in the irresistible stench of its water, insomuch that when it finds itself in danger from an enemy, it moistens its tail plentifully with this liquid ammunition and with great fury sprinkles it like a shower of rain full into the eyes of its assailant. By this it gains time to make its escape.' [24]

But with all his half-facetious notices about animals and his neighbors, Byrd was never unmindful of his obligations to Providence. 'In this great and solitary wilderness we had all along been fed by Heaven,' he says, and in remembrance thereof the men agreed to wear on their chests the figure of a turkey cock with its wings extended. The fowl held in its claws a scroll bearing the motto *Vice coturnicum*, 'meaning that we had been supported by them in the wilderness in the room of quails.'

He even went so far as to put down his views on keeping the Sabbath, by way of reminding his reader, if reminding was necessary, that none of his jests was to be taken as implying a disrespect for morality.

I would not be thought so rigid an observer of the Sabbath as to allow no work at all to be done, or journeys to be taken upon it. I should not care to lie still and be knocked in the head, as the Jews were heretofore by Antiochus, because I believed it unlawful to stand upon my defense on this good day. Nor would I care, like a certain New England magistrate, to order a man to a whipping post for daring to ride for a midwife on the Lord's day. On the contrary I am for doing all acts of necessity, charity, and self-preservation upon a Sunday as well as other days of the week.

He was equally serious regarding His Majesty's interest in 'the grand ledge of mountains' to the west of Virginia and Carolina, lest 'our good friends the French' possess it themselves and form an alliance with the Indians. He suspected that valuable silver and gold deposits lay hidden within this district. And it was a dire reproach on his countrymen to think that, after inhabiting their colony close to one hundred and thirty years, they 'hardly knew anything of the Appalachian mountains that are nowhere above two hundred and fifty miles from the sea.' [25] The

French, 'who are later comers,' on the other hand, had meanwhile 'ranged from Quebec southward as far as the mouth of the Mississippi, and to the west almost as far as California, which is either way above two thousand miles.' This truth, soberly threatening, seems to have worried him as long as he lived.

The last weeks of the expedition would likely have been lean ones but for Bearskin's good marksmanship. He managed to kill a bear or so each day, which furnished the company with a very desirable diet.

And now [Byrd wrote, near the conclusion of his book], for the good of mankind and for the better peopling an infant colony which has no want but that of inhabitants, I will venture to publish a secret of importance our Indian disclosed to me. I asked him the reason why few or none of his countrywomen were barren. To this curious question he answered, with a broad grin upon his face, they had an infallible secret for that. Upon my being importunate to know what the secret might be, he informed me that, if any Indian woman did not prove with child at a decent time after marriage, the husband, to save his reputation with the women, forthwith entered into a bear diet for six weeks, which in that time makes him so vigorous that he grows exceedingly impertinent to his poor wife, and 'tis great odds but he makes her a mother in nine months.

And thus I am able to say, besides, for the reputation of the bear diet, that all the married men of our company were joyful fathers within forty weeks after they got home, and most of the single men had children sworn to them within the same time, our chaplain only excepted who, with much ado, made shift to cast out that importunate kind of devil by dint of fasting and prayer.[26]

Byrd's choice of the phrase 'within forty weeks after they got home' was considerably more deliberate than might at first appear. Had he augmented this limit to forty-five, he would have confessed his own indebtedness to the diet. For at the end of that interval his wife bore him his fourth child in as many years, little Jane. And, oddly enough, she was his last.

X

TRAVELER IN EDEN

And that night, with its autumnal richness still fresh in memory he dreamed 'of the delights of Tempe and the Elysian fields.'

I

VIRGINIA's colonial aristocracy could never afford to be too exclusive. To be exclusive implies self-sufficiency. One must be able to move altogether in circles whose identity resembles one's own. Aristocracy always appears, in consequence, somewhat of an anomaly where pioneering is still in evidence, for common dangers and similar natural difficulties induce an essential fraternalism. Byrd and his fellow Councillors had managed, by divers forms of reciprocal favoritism, to create for themselves a certain property nobility. Their several strong boxes contained lieutenant-governors' deeds to thousands upon thousands of acres. By 1732, a very considerable fraction of the best land in Virginia had been thus narrowly distributed, and Byrd, one may feel sure, had not failed to get his share.

But such widely scattered holdings demanded a vast amount of looking after, and it was in conducting this personal supervision that the aristocratic tradition broke down. To effect the task properly, in Byrd's case, required a month at least — thirty days of sleeping with overseers and their children in one-room cabins, of slushing through marshes, and eating bear meat without the delicacy of 'anything farinaceous' to render this monotonous nourishment palatable. One's supper often depended upon an Indian hunter's good marksmanship and industry. Both virtues were necessary, and Byrd at times complained that after killing an animal the natives would balk at the task of carrying it to camp, giving as an excuse that it was too lean to warrant so much trouble. Such insolence wrought grievously with Byrd's pretensions to dignity and made a democratic sense of humor his only recourse. Fortunately he had this trait in abundance; and his remaining journals, *A Progress to the Mines* and *A Journey to Eden*, which are records of two of these overseeing trips, show that it served him in excellent stead.

Byrd undertook his Progress to the Mines in September and October, 1732. He was concerned, in this instance, not only with informing himself of the condition of his property, but also with acquiring some statistics on the cost of iron manufacture. For that reason he set out with Spotswood's home as his destination. Old political differences between the two men had long been forgotten, and the former Lieutenant-Governor, as everybody knew, had done more in the mining business than anyone else in the colonies. Byrd quite evidently intended, if desirable property could be found, to venture into this curious industry himself. But he knew little about it, and having often seen how strangely men's enthusiasm over new ventures usurped their judgment and precipitated indebtedness, he was skeptical from the start.

With his wife and 'her little governor, my son,' who accompanied him a short way, Byrd set out in his chariot. Together they journeyed some fifteen miles, until noon, and then halted 'by a purling stream and picked the bones of a piece of roast beef.' [1] The lunch gave him courage, he said, to make the rest of the journey alone on horseback. At his first stop, his father's old place near the falls of the James, he found things in a bad way. 'It had rained so little for many weeks that the Naides had hardly water enough left to wash their faces.'

Byrd began at once setting everything possible to rights. Certain blasting had to be done. He left directions with the miller, imparted a little of 'Minerva's inspiration' to the weaver, looked about unsuccessfully for iron, and went in finally to consider his overseer's wife, a 'Caledonian spinster who, since my last visit, had mended more in her looks than in her humour.' Byrd found the lady much too high-spirited for his 'first minister.' He believed that a man should rule without question in his own household and, upon his departure, informed this gentleman to that effect. 'I told him I could not pity a man who had it always in his power to do himself and her justice and would not. If she were a drunkard, a scold, a thief or a slanderer, we had wholesome laws that would make her back smart for the diversion of her other members, and 'twas his fault if he had not put these wholesome severities into execution.' [2]

The following morning, after tossing down his poached eggs 'with as much ease as some good breeders slip children into the world,' Byrd crossed the river. His next stop was at Colonel Randolph's at Tuckahoe. Rain delayed him here several days, along with Mrs. Fleming, another friend of his host. This lady's husband was absent. He had moved on to Goochland, and she was impatient to follow him. 'I said what I could to comfort a gentlewoman under so sad a disappointment,' Byrd notes, 'and told her that it was prudent for married people to fast sometimes for one another that they might come together again with the better stomach.' [3]

While there, he was visited by the parish minister. Here was another male dominated by a shrewish wife. 'The gray mare is clearly the better horse in his family, and the poor man submits to her wild vagaries for peace's sake.' These intimate details Byrd of course learned from Mrs. Fleming as soon as their guest had departed.

But the rain continued throughout the following day, trying 'both Mrs. Fleming's patience and my own good breeding.' Seeing that his leisure would probably be prolonged, he endeavored 'to find out what subject a dull married man could introduce that might best bring the lady to the use of her tongue.' Soon he discovered that she was a notable quack, and they talked about the bloody flux at great length. But the conversation finally became too grave, Byrd feared. He began to chat of plays, 'and finding her taste lay most towards comedy, I offered to read her one, which she kindly accepted.'

She produced Part II of *The Beggar's Opera*. Byrd explained how this play had 'diverted the town' for forty nights successively and gained forty-five hundred pounds for the author, and how its chief interest lay in the timeliness of its satirical references to the ministry, then out of favor. He read three acts and, the sky having cleared, left Mrs. Fleming and Randolph to finish it. 'Thus we killed the time,' he wrote, 'and triumphed over the bad weather.' [4]

Byrd stopped next at a Mr. Chiswell's. Here he was 'very handsomely entertained, finding everything very clean and very good' — a detail which, if true, he never failed to mention. But Mrs. Chiswell, an old friend of his bachelor days, was aged to such an extent as to take much of the joy from his visit. 'It was impossible to know her again, so much the flower had faded.' And yet, he confesses, though she had grown an old woman, 'she was one of those absolute rarities, a very good old woman.'

Chiswell, who had lost heavily in the mining business, imparted much valuable advice on the subject to Byrd. The important consideration, he believed, was the distance from the mine to a navigable waterway. One hundred and twenty slaves were necessary to carry on the business. These laborers would require sixteen hundred barrels of corn yearly to support them. Two square miles of virgin forest would supply the furnace with fuel timber. A moderate-sized plant would run about eight hundred tons of pig iron a year, and the clear profit one could expect in England would approximate four pounds per ton. The operator could therefore depend on some thirty-two hundred pounds yearly in return for his initial investment, land, and negroes.

He carefully noted these several items in his journal, and then went to his lodging for the night. He always drank a tonic of Jesuit's bark, or quinine, before bedtime. On this occasion he had to take it in water, 'by reason a light-fingered damsel had ransacked my baggage and drunk up my brandy.' The next day he and his host exchanged brewing secrets; discussed new ways of keeping weevils from wheat; dined upon venison 'as fat and well tasted as if it had come out of Richmond park,' a place near London; looked over Chiswell's mill, where Byrd observed the surprising fact that those negroes employed there 'which are kept barest of cloathes and bedding are commonly the freest from sickness.' This latter observation he was reluctant to make 'for fear of encouraging cruelty.' [5]

Together these gentlemen rode on to the mines at Fredericksville. Byrd lists an imposing number of other facts about metallurgy. The furnace had to be heated six weeks in order to reach the necessary smelting point. A total expenditure of twelve thousand pounds was required before the business became profitable. Statistics about the cost of coal, felling the wood to be used, the weight of 'two mighty pair of bellows,' land, negroes, cattle, and ways to reduce the iron's brittleness follow in an ill-digested jumble. Byrd's ignorance of the subject appears uniformly complete, but it must be said that he took the most sensible method imaginable of informing himself.

It seems that the significant item in influencing him to stay out of the business was Chiswell's opinion that Parliament would soon expressly forbid the colonies to manufacture finished iron products of any sort. Byrd realized at once that this was the most lucrative phase of the industry. Yet he also knew enough about the home government to see that its ministers recognized the impetus to independence which would follow upon the colonies setting up manufactures of their own. The finished product had to come from England. Otherwise, as one has seen, a trading vessel sent from the mother country to Virginia would be empty on the voyage over, and half the trip would, in consequence, have to be made without profit. The politics and economics of the situation were both absurdly simple.

Having learned nearly all Chiswell had to impart, Byrd rode on to Spotswood's place at Germanna. There he spent the first evening 'talking over a legend of old stories until it was time for the traveler to retire.' Byrd let his friend know the next morning that 'besides the pleasure of paying him a visit, I came to be instructed by so great a master in the mystery of making of iron, wherein you lead the way and are the Tubal Cain of Virginia.' This compliment proved far from comprehensive enough. Spotswood corrected Byrd 'by assuring me that he was not only the first in this colony but the first in North America who had erected a regular furnace.' [6]

The afternoon, meetly enough, was devoted to the ladies, in particular to Miss Theky, Mrs. Spotswood's sister. This gentlewoman showed Byrd around the garden. He noted especially a bench where she 'often sat and bewailed her virginity.' Again they were up until it was almost morning, drinking prosperity to all Spotswood's projects. But their conversation with the ladies was 'like whip sillibub, very pretty, but nothing to it.'

The next day was Miss Theky's birthday 'upon which I made her my compliments and wished she might live twice as long a married woman as she had a maid. I did not presume to pry into the secret of her age, nor was she forward to disclose it, lest I should think her wisdom fell short of her years.' [7]

But more talk about iron followed. Byrd alternately played the gallant and took notes on mining. He regarded the former exercise as apparently something of a necessary evil. Admiring Mrs. Spotswood's 'little animals' was naturally a considerable exaction, when his real intent had been to learn about a business in which he hoped to retrieve his sunken fortunes.

It is apparent that administrative policies of the mother country were not wholly indorsed by this former Lieutenant-Governor and his guest of the Council of Virginia. Their conversation, as Byrd notes it, reflects a well-ingrained contempt for the integrity of the royal ministers. Taxes paid into their hands seemed 'to molder away between their fingers.' The New-Englanders were still contributing certain revenues into the home treasury. They should 'stand bluff' and refuse. If the Crown tried to force payment, it would find the task difficult. The colonists had not voted this assessment themselves and, Byrd declared prophetically, 'it is against the rights of Englishmen to be taxed but by their representatives.' [8]

Another phase of the matter was seen in Byrd's experience with hemp. The King promised a bounty upon all this commodity raised in Virginia, but he also demanded the right of refusal when the product was put on sale. Nearly always it was bought for the navy, and the poor planter had to wait so long for the government to pay him his price and bonus that his capital was soon exhausted. Plainly there was something ominous in the air, when two such conservatives as these appeared so outspoken.

Byrd's visit lasted six days. After his departure he met one of the former Lieutenant-Governor's managers, 'who complained that Spotswood starves his works out of whimsicalness and frugality, endeavoring to do everything with his own people, and at the same time taking them off upon every vagary that comes into his head.' [9] Byrd is not averse throughout his journals to noting the inadequacies of his hosts. But he is usually less detached in his other works. Here his comments are chiefly objective, to be taken on their own merit. This absence of a dominant personal bias makes *A Progress to the Mines* the least interesting of his journals, for in obscuring his own prejudice he omits an essential of satire.

Byrd journeyed home very much as he had come. He learned more about iron, a new method of preparing tobacco, heard much scandal regarding the neighbors of those with whom he stopped, and visited another of his plantations. Here he spent a night with a widow, Mrs. Syms, who failed to recognize him. 'This lady, at first suspecting I was some lover, put on a gravity that becomes a weed. She was a portly dame of the family of Esau and seemed not to pine too much for the death of her husband, who was of the family of the Saracens. He left a son by her, who had all the strong features of his sire, so that the most malicious of her neighbors can't bring his legitimacy into question.' [10] After discoursing at some length upon his affairs, Byrd retired to his room 'and rehearsed all the follys of the day, the little I had learnt and still less good I had done.'

But absence had made him long 'for the delights of my own family, for the smiles of an affectionate wife, and the prattle of my innocent children.' His stay at this last place was as brief as possible, and his delight quite as considerable when, upon reaching home, 'I had the great satisfaction to find all that was dearest to me in good health.'

2

Byrd set out upon his journey to the Land of Eden in September, 1733. His company consisted of some ten fellow travelers whose mission was that of looking over and surveying certain of their respective outlying plantations and of applying for any new, especially desirable territory they might discover.

His first stop was at Mayor Mumford's, 'who made me the compliment to leave the arms of a pretty wife to lie on the cold ground for my sake.' There they met another companion, Peter Jones, fortified themselves with a beefsteak, 'kissed our landlady for good luck,' and departed. A few miles further on, two other members of the party joined them. Major Embry, their host for the evening, was ill of a fever, but Byrd prescribed for him a gallon or two of chicken broth that 'washed him as clear as a gun.' The next day the entire company, 'after cheering our hearts with three bottles of pretty good madeira,' moved on toward the backwoods.

Byrd's eye was still open to whatever signs he could encounter of silver, copper, or iron mines. But he was as skeptical as ever of the possibilities of finding anything of value. When the rumor that some ore had been discovered was whispered about, he wrote, the inhabitants of the community seemed all to go 'mine mad, and neglect the making of corn for their present necessities in hopes of growing very rich hereafter.'

The travelers stopped the first night at a friend's outlying plantation. 'Our fare there was pretty coarse, but Mr. Banister and I took possession of the bed while the rest of the company lay in bulk upon the floor. That night,' he notes, 'the little major [Banister] made the first discovery of an impatient and peevish temper, equally unfit both for a traveler and a husband.' [11] The following

evening their accommodations at one of Byrd's plantations were quite as bad. 'My overseer, Harry Morris, did
his utmost to entertain me and my company. The worst
of it was that we were obliged all to be littered down in one
room, along with my landlady and four children, one of
whom was very sick and consequently very fretful.' [12] The
natural unpleasantness of this situation was aggravated
by this same lady, who 'discovered some broad signs of
the fury by breaking out into insolent and passionate
expressions against the poor negroes.' Byrd sagely concluded that if his presence could not awe her, 'she could be
very outrageous when I was an hundred miles off.'

The nineteenth of September, eight days after the expedition started, is a memorable date. Because he 'de-
tested idleness,' Byrd had been out for some time with his
overseer at the falls of the James, looking over certain
new entries for land he had made in that neighborhood.
'When we got home,' he notes, 'we laid the foundation of
two large cities: one at Shacco's, to be called Richmond,
and the other at the point of the Appomattuck River, to
be named Petersburg.' The latter city was so designated
after a local inhabitant, Richmond from its fancied resemblance to a town of the same name near London.
Byrd was quick to recognize that, since these places were
situated at the uppermost landings of the two rivers, they
were 'naturally intended for marts, where the traffic of
the outer inhabitants must center.' He had seen that this
was so even in childhood. The vessels that came there,
bringing merchandise to his father, invariably had to turn
back after delivering them. It was the end of the tidewater. 'Thus,' he concluded, 'did we build cities in the air.'

But they did not remain in the air long. Hard pressed by debt, Byrd put his Richmond lots on sale in 1737.

This is to give notice [ran his advertisement in the *Virginia Gazette*] that on the north side of James River, near the upper-most landing... is lately laid off a town with streets sixty-five feet wide, in a pleasant and healthy situation and well supplied with springs of good water.... The lots will be granted in fee simple on condition only of building a house in three years time of twenty-four by sixteen feet, fronting within five feet of the street. The lots to be rated according to the convenience of their situation and sold after this April General Court by me,

WILLIAM BYRD [13]

The party rode on, now approaching the North Carolina backwoods in good earnest. Byrd waded through water 'so high that it ran into the top of my boots,' feasted at one meal 'upon a young buck that had the ill luck to cross our way,' fasted at the next because a rainstorm continually extinguished his fire, and proved himself a good sports-man in every emergency. 'My greatest disaster,' he writes, 'was that in mounting a precipice my steed made a short turn and gave my knee an unmerciful bang against a tree, and I felt the effects of it several days after.' But this brought about no interruption to the journey. He 'went merrily on.' Three days later, he says, though the injury was no better, 'I broke not the laws of traveling by uttering the least complaint.'

In truth, Byrd had need of his self-composure else-where. No sooner had his little company reached the dividing line and pitched their tent for the night than a woodsman discovered unmistakable signs of a recent Indian encampment. It was evident that the natives had moved on only the day before. The entire group was soon in an uproar. 'I put as good a countenance upon the matter as I could,' he assures us, recalling the incident in the security of his home, 'informing my fellow travelers that these Northern Indians were at peace with us, and although one or two of them may now and then commit a robbery or murder (as other rogues do), yet nationally and avowedly they would not venture to hurt us.' [14] But this talk of national peace and integrity was quite too specious to allay their several fears at that particular moment. Byrd so far admits this as to say that the fright 'took the edge off our appetites for everything but the rum bottle, which was more in favor than ever because of its cordial quality.' [15]

His party was quite willing to move on at daybreak, though no further signs of Indians were discovered. Before nightfall they had crossed the line and had reached the Land of Eden. Byrd ordered a survey to begin at once. He wrote with peculiar enthusiasm about the excellence of this tract. Here was 'a delightful situation for the manor house.' Farther on a creek forked and its western branch 'was wide enough to merit the name of river.' 'Charming peninsulas' thrust graceful arms into the stream. Where hills were stony and barren, Byrd's jubilation, for the first time of which there is any record, ran high in expectancy of 'the riches that might lie underground.'

There were agreeable pauses in the surveying work. During one of them 'several of us plunged into the river, notwithstanding it was a frosty morning.' One of the Indians went along with these gentlemen and taught them a thing about swimming. 'They strike not out both hands together,' Byrd notes, but alternately one after another, 'whereby they are able to swim both farther and faster than we do.' [16]

Under the spell of this rare environment Byrd's heart expanded to compass in its magnanimity all poor wretches less fortunate than himself. There is a blind tradition amongst the Indians, he writes, 'that work was first laid upon mankind by the female, and therefore 'tis but just that that sex should do the greatest part of it.' This was merely pretense to him. 'The true explanation is that the weakest must always go to the wall, and superiority has from the beginning ungenerously imposed slavery on those who are not able to resist it.' But this sage observation from a rather considerable slave-holder can scarcely be interpreted as his guiding conviction.

Byrd may not have been in philosophic accord with slavery. Indeed, he wrote an associate of Oglethorpe, the Earl of Egmont, praising him in no uncertain terms for excluding negroes from Georgia.

I am sensible [he went on to say] of many bad consequences of multiplying these Ethiopians amongst us. They blow up the pride and ruin the industry of our white people, who, seeing a rank of poor creatures below them, detest work for fear it should make them look like slaves. Then that poverty, which will ever attend upon idleness, disposes them as much to pilfer as it does the Portuguese, who account it much more like a gentleman to steal than to dirty their hands with labor of any kind.

Another unhappy effect of many negroes is the necessity of being severe. Numbers make them insolent, and then foul means must do what fair will not. And even this is terrible to a good-natured man, who must submit to be either a fool or a fury. And this will be more our unhappy case, the more the negroes are increased.

But these private mischiefs are nothing, if compared to the public danger. We have already at least ten thousand men of these descendants of Ham fit to bear arms, and these numbers increase every day, as well by birth as by importation. And in case there should arise a man of desperate courage here, exasperated by a desperate fortune, he might with more advantage than Catiline kindle a servile war. It were therefore worth the consideration of a British Parliament, my Lord, to put an end to this unchristian traffick of making merchandise of our fellow creatures.[17]

Yet if Byrd really did fear some ultimate danger to English supremacy through a negro revolt, or through their uniting with the French, as he elsewhere suggested, he was far too completely a civilized product of his age to do anything about it. Men may have their ideas, may think as radically as they like, for that matter, but men, he believed, should also recognize the futility of opposing in actual conduct anything so dully amenable to change as convention. Such policies brought discord and upheavals into the world. They involved one's setting one's self against the majority of one's fellows and trying to impose upon them some system for which they were unprepared and unwilling to accept. Byrd would no more consider making such an anomaly of himself than he would consider dressing untidily, or out of accord with the latest available fashion. It was far simpler and pleasanter to be regarded as intellectually advanced, and to content one's self with that.

The surveying soon over, Byrd's party turned back toward their homes. He could not quit this pleasant situation, he says, referring to his land, 'without regret, and often faced about to take a parting look at it as far as I could see, and so indeed did all the rest of the company.' And that night, with its autumnal richness still fresh in memory, he dreamt 'of the delights of Tempe and the Elysian fields.'

The journey henceforth was vastly less pleasant, as might be suspected of any going away from Eden. One of the men, a drone who loved to do little and eat much and who 'was never in humour unless his belly was full,' had squandered away his bread. He began to break the rules of traveling by complaining and threatening to desert. Another 'had a small fever and bore it like a child: He groaned as if he had been in labor and thought verily it would be his fate to die like a mutinous Israelite in the wilderness and be buried under a heap of stones.' [18]

Food became scarce, their bread was exhausted, and they 'lived upon venison and bear 'till our stomachs loathed them almost as much as the Hebrews of old did their quails.' They followed the wrong branch of a stream and were lost. 'We called it Jesuit's creek,' Byrd says, 'because it misled us.'

But this confusion was relieved at intervals. Once a buffalo crossed their way and they dined on its tongue and udder, 'which were so good that a cardinal legate might have made a comfortable meal upon them during the carnival.' Another time they camped on the same spot where the dividing-line party had spent a night five years before. 'The beech whose bark recorded the names of the Carolina commissioners was still standing, and we did them the justice to add to their names a sketch of their characters.' [19] They stopped occasionally for time sufficient to assist other members of the party in surveying tracts of land previously entered for. And on one occasion, at least, Byrd gave his entire company an apparently novel lesson in applied dentistry.

He suddenly found himself 'with an impertinent tooth in my upper jaw,' which made grinding a biscuit a matter of much deliberation and presence of mind. He decided to get rid of the troublesome member 'by cutting a caper.' After causing a twine to be fastened round its root, he tied the other end to a log in such a way that he could barely stand upright. 'Having adjusted my string in this manner, I bent my knees enough to enable me to spring vigorously off the ground. The force of the leap drew out the tooth with so much ease that I felt nothing of it, nor would have believed it was come away unless I had seen it dangling at the end of the string.' [20] For the benefit of those unacquainted with this 'new way of tooth drawing,' Byrd adds that 'an under tooth may be fetched out in the same manner by standing off the ground and fastening the string a due distance above you.'

They were now nearing the homes of the more remotely settled members of the party, and 'returning to that evil custom of lying in a house' — evil indeed 'when ten or a dozen people are forced to pig together in a room, as we did, and are troubled with the squalling of peevish, dirty children into the bargain.' Byrd stopped at another of his plantations for the night. 'We ate our fill of potatoes, which seemed delicious fare to those who have made a campaign in the woods.'

But it is evident that this place was being grossly mismanaged. He confesses that he was forced to threaten his overseer 'with my highest displeasure, unless he mended his conduct very much. I also let him know that he was not only to correct his own errors, but likewise those of his wife, since the power certainly belonged to him, in virtue of his conjugal authority.' [21] But here again, it seemed, was a situation wherein 'the gray mare appeared the better horse,' and Byrd suspected, even as he gave it, that this last admonition would be futile.

As he neared his own home, hilarity superseded other less becoming virtues and with the remnant of the party he celebrated the success of their trip. Once, 'in the gaiety of our hearts,' he says, 'we drank our bottle a little too freely, which had an unusual effect on persons so long accustomed to simple element.' It appears that Byrd and his host, Mr. Banister, were raised out of their separate beds at the same moment by one of the more elementary urges to which mortality is subject. To Byrd, this incident was indicative, suggesting a scientific truth of far-reaching implications. He regarded it as fair proof 'that people who breathe the same air and are engaged in the same way of living [as had been the case with himself and Banister during the past month] will be very apt to fall into the same indispositions. And this may explain why distempers sometimes go round a family, without any reason to believe they are infectious, according to the superstition of the vulgar.' [22]

GRAYING CAVALIER

Futility was in the wind that fanned his face and swelled the white sails growing smaller in the distance. And he would walk back into his house in bitterness, because of a debt that would not be thrown off, for all his planning, and scheming, and prayer.

I

WESTOVER was probably finished by 1736. It was a house upon which Byrd lavished his resources, for he meant to be proud of it. There it stood on a high bluff, the central building of three stories crowned by a steeply sloping roof. On either side of this structure extended the smaller gambrel-topped wings. Farther on, and considerably more to the rear, stretched the servants' quarters, glistening with recent whitewash, and the more impressive rooms of the overseer and of Mr. Procter. Still more removed, and leading always to the rear, were stables, with the wide fields beyond.

The lines of the main building were simple almost to severity. Its brick was plain. It had no porch. Generally, one might term it a Georgian variant of many a home Byrd had visited in London. More particularly, it bore a close resemblance to Drayton Court, Northamptonshire, residence of the late Earl of Petersborough.[1]

Running the full depth of the interior of the house was the great hall, eighteen feet wide. Near the end a stairway ascended, its twisted balustrades of mahogany brought over especially from London. The drawing-room, with its rich paneling and gilded ceiling, was dominated by the

DRAWING-ROOM AT WESTOVER

Showing black-and-white marble mantel imported by Colonel Byrd

black-and-white Italian marble mantel. Byrd had imported this, along with practically all his other furniture.

But a stranger to the colonies would likely have been
quite amazed by the cellars of Westover. The entire mansion was underrun with them. Beneath one there was a
secret room. Others, usually some eight feet square, all
strangely wound about to converge at last, so tradition
informs, at the subterranean passage that led down to the
river. This tunnel was planned to afford a means of escape
from possible Indian raids. Two other underground rooms,
also hiding-places, might be reached through a dry well.
One of these connected directly with a bedchamber on the
third story. Horace Walpole or Monk Lewis might well
have planned a Gothic romance amid such a labyrinth of
dark enclosures. Byrd used them exclusively to store his
claret and madeira in.

In front of the house, hardly a hundred yards, the broad
blue James moved quietly to the sea. Beyond the wing on
the right was the low, walled-in two-acre garden, already
known as the most famous in the colony for the abundance
of rare flowers and herbs growing there. It was in one of
the shaded corners of this place that, before very long,
Evelyn was to be buried.

But now it was summer, and the tall oaks and maples
and elm trees before the house blanketed the lawn with
shade. And what a commotion was rampant inside! In
Byrd's phrase 'the seasons had brought in the ships,' and
with them, letters from home.

There was no hope for rest at Westover this day! Why,
in London they were playing 'a certain game upon the
cards called whist, and it has engaged the men of all ages to

keep company with women more than ever anything did
before. 'Tis apparent there are much stronger charms belonging to cards than any of the female sex can boast of.' [2]
Men are spending six evenings a week in the company of
women; they have even ceased to be drunk; that is, people
of fashion have, and doubtless other vice is abating in
consequence.

But Cousin Taylor must leave this subject to tell of a
conquest she had made when last at Tunbridge, 'at the
same time owning what a fool I was not to snap at such a
lumping prize. This great and weighty man passed on un-
regarded by me amongst the crowd, though, I was afterwards informed, suffered greatly to see me play so much.
In reality it had well-nigh hindered his proposal, had not
love got the better of his fears. But to draw towards a
conclusion, I was fool enough to think myself happier in
my own little way of life than I should have been with such
eminent riches. But the sequel of the story is moving indeed, for this good man (who was doubtless fit for heaven)
God Almighty took to himself in little more than a year
afterwards, and as I now can neither dishonor him nor
spoil his future preferment, I will venture to tell you he
was no less a person than Sir Francis Child.' [3]

Sir Francis Child! Head of the proverbially great bank-
ing firm of Francis Child and Company, never once married, and Lord Mayor of London! Poor Cousin Taylor.
Here was substance for a week's conversation, and
lamenting.

Byrd had worked out a plan, he once told Sister Otway,
of preserving a semblance of peace at his home when
letters such as this one arrived.

We tear them open [he confessed] as eagerly as a greedy heir tears open a rich father's will. But as no pleasure derived from this imperfect world flows clear to us, so every time Mrs. Byrd hears from any of you she sleeps no more the livelong night. Therefore I find it necessary, when my English letters come to hand late in the day, to pocket 'em up until next morning. Thus when madam has the whole day before her, perhaps her joy will evaporate so far as to allow some rest. In this prudent manner female passions require to be managed sometimes, to confine them in bounds and keep them, like a high mettled horse, from running away with their owners.[4]

Though Byrd, as far as is known, was never visited at Westover by any of the English relatives with whom he corresponded so intimately, guests of the colonies were frequent. At his home they found the lavish colonial hospitality which fiction for the past century has pictured with such nostalgic approbation. Calls would be protracted for weeks at a time. No matter who the visitor, he represented something of the vast outside and little-known world, a sort of animate newspaper, certain to impart his store of information.

If only once some sojourner at Westover had, when he left, written an account of his stay there! Surely there were house-parties enough. From up and down the river guests would come, rowed by singing servants. Overland from Williamsburg they would come too — notables all — in their silks, and satins, and laces: Spotswood, perhaps, from far-off Germanna, even John Custis, long a woman-hater, the Carters from Shirley, the Harrisons from Brandon, Patrick Henry's father, and Sir John Randolph, whose memories of London were nearly as glamorous as Byrd's own.

An atmosphere of elegant informality won the visitor as soon as he arrived. There was dancing continuously, morning, afternoon, and evening. Out across the blue waters of the James, the faint strains of violins drifted lazily. Romance was awake in the garden, in the summer house, the hawthornes about it still white with blossoms. And there were trim borders of boxwood lining the walks, banked depths of honeysuckle, and larkspur and jasmine and clustered roses and pinks. The air was heavy with their fragrance, rich with the poignant sadness of spring.

About the supper-table, after the ladies had withdrawn, the more mature gentlemen talked of world affairs and sipped Antigua rum poured from stately decanters. War with Spain or with France was the political subject of conversation always uppermost. These two nations, as long as they held territory to the north, south, and west, were a constant menace to the seaboard colonies. But they also talked horses and taxes, of the runaway servant problem, of excluding North Carolina tobacco from Virginia ports, of the satires of Swift and the couplets of Mr. Pope.

During the course of their stay, visitors found many ways of diverting themselves. Some might ride over the grounds with Byrd. Others might join in a fox hunt. Still others might, more or less informally, race their prize horses, if they had brought them, for imposing sums. There was always at least one table of cards, with a bowl of lime toddy conveniently near. The dancing hardly ever stopped. But if he preferred, the more scholarly friend might retire for an hour to the library.

Then there were always Byrd's portraits to enjoy — Southwell's, the Earl of Orrery's, the Marquis of Halifax's,

Patty Blount's, Lord Egmont's, Cousin Taylor's, his own children's. He had ranged them down his stately hallway, nearly all the work of Kneller at his best. This much of the past he had been able to save from the insolence of Time.

Not all the entertaining Byrd did at Westover took place on such a grand scale. There were frequent visits by this or that intimate friend and his family. These were still more informal, but quite as interesting. And if the guest happened to be so admired an acquaintance as Randolph, Byrd would be writing him to come again almost the moment he and his family had departed:

Dear Sir:

In hopes you may be safe at Williamsburg by this time and my lady up to the elbow in Sausages and Black Puddings, I can't forbear greeting you well, and signifying our joy at your arrival in your own chimney corner. We have had the good nature to be in pain for you ever since you left us, though in good truth your obstinacy in exposing your wife and children to be starved with cold and buried in the mire, hardly deserved it. No doubt you were obliged to have Pioneers to clean the way before you as far as Mr. Custis's plantation, and you needed four yoke of oxen, as they do in the deep roads of Sussex, to drag you through the dirt. I dare say notwithstanding your fine horses you were not able to go along faster than Mr. Attorney walks.... Upon the news of Mrs. Stagg's death, Madame la Baronne de Graffenreid is in hopes to succeed to part of her business in town. And were it not for making my good lady jealous (which I would not do for the world) I would recommend her to your favor. She really takes abundance of pains and teaches well, and were you to attack her virtue you would find her chaste as Lucretia.

We are told there is a Bristol ship arrived at York River. If she brings any news be so good as to communicate it to your country friends, and in case you should have nothing foreign we should be glad of a little domestic, which of your actors shone most in the play next Isabinda, who, I take it for granted, is the Oldfield of the theatre. How came Squire Marplot off? With many a clap I suppose, though I fancy he would have acted more to life in the comedy called the Sham Doctor. But not a word of this for fear in case of sickness he might poison or revenge your humble servant,

WM. BYRD [5]

From the year 1736 onward, Byrd was never cut off from regular information about life beyond his own estate. He was indebted for this improved state of affairs, as has been suggested, to Mr. William Parks, of Maryland, who had moved over to Williamsburg, set up a printing-office, and begun the publication of his weekly *Virginia Gazette*. Parks was an apostle of culture. He printed poems and essays as often as political news. He advertised books. He announced problems in mathematics and offered prizes for their solution. And his four-page paper, especially when there were no visitors, was enthusiastically welcomed by the news-loving family at Westover.

But when Byrd wanted more permanent literary satisfaction or entertainment than a newspaper was able to afford, he could find it readily in his library. Here, indeed, was an oasis one would hardly have expected to discover in the colonies. Thirty-six hundred volumes of history, divinity, travel, philosophy, poetry, law — there they all were, ranged about a spacious side room in solemn, silent impressiveness, all neatly catalogued by his amusing librarian, Mr. Procter.

Today Byrd might find a communication from this gentleman on the table before him — a very scurvy writing surely — to the effect that there were no more candles in his room, and that though he took a folio from the library to read at night for his own betterment, he was puzzled to know how his master expected this to be done without illumination. Moreover, the complaint continued, there were no tongs in his house, and when necessity required a fire he was at a palpable disadvantage.

Byrd sat down and answered the letter forthwith:

Most Hypocondriack Sir:

I have your list of complaints, which you drew up in the form of a letter, I suppose, to save blushing. As to your being often forced, like mad people, to sit in the dark without a candle, I have this to say, that orders have been given from the beginning to furnish you with one every night, and if these orders have at any time been disobeyed, upon the least complaint from you that grievance would have been redresst. But I understand the candles are not big enough for you. I am sorry we have not wax, or at least mould candles to light you in your lucubrations. Had your dear friend Mr. Stephens supplied us with more tallow, perhaps we might have been better able to light up the white house with bigger candles. In the meantime, if such as you have, by the judgment of two good men, will burn an hour and a half, that is full long enough to read by candle light, which is not good for the eyes, and after that, meditation and devotion might fill up the rest of an evening. Then as to the calamity of your wanting those useful implements of tongs and poker, that I must own, is a very compassionate case. But I can clear myself of this impeachment too, for I remember I ordered the smith to make a pair of tongs on purpose for you, and if you or your chamber fellow unluckily destroyed them, it was by no means the fault of

Yours

WM. BYRD [6]

But for all his complaining, Procter was thoroughly

satisfied with his situation at Westover and confessed the
fact freely to relatives in Europe:

I serve a very honorable and virtuous master — for the time
being I live as happily, if not it is my own fault, as my worthy
master himself. He is very communicative in conversation and
lets me enjoy that of strangers as much as may well be. I am
library keeper, and have all genteel conveniences; moreover, to
save me a risk he gives me a draught upon his London factor,
and orders my clothes with his own goods at the English price —
besides the kindness of the family in often having my linen made
and mended.... For my future advantage Col. Byrd will certainly procure me a parish of £100 sterling a year, if I can like it,
or keep me to commence as husbandman upon land of my own.
My good master, indeed, frequently is pleasant with me and says
wh'nt I be at once a parson and a planter.[7]

In this library, one would think, Byrd had traveled
imaginatively over the entire known world. It was in his
books that he found that freedom which the accumulating
years told him must be experienced vicariously or relinquished forever. And what places people had sailed to or
written about! Here were voyages to Abyssinia, *Travels of
the Jesuits*, *A voyage to Cartesius' world*, Magellan's *China*,
an account of Macasar, a voyage to Moscovie, and a description of the Isle of Orkney. More travels and journeys
by LeGreat, Sales, Hennepin, Cooke, Ray, and Drake
were there, whole sets of miscellaneous voyages, Walker's
expedition to Canada, a trip to Jerusalem, to the Canary
Islands and to St. Kilda. It was small wonder that Byrd
could write about the Hottentots of Cape Cod, or discuss
the Italian tarantula with such impressiveness.

Travelers in his day were 'curious' men indeed, attracted as much by quaint phenomena as by the dryly

scientific. There were so many places to sail to of which
few people had heard. The world was so often revealing a
new aspect of itself, surprising, often amazing, the naïve
creatures who lived upon it. It was the age of which
Newton had spoken, when men were still finding, as it
were, quaint shells upon the shore, and leaving the
tedious work of synthesis and classification to later and
more crabbed generations.

Then there was his medical collection, historically ar-
ranged, from the *Aphorisms and Commentaries* of Hippo-
crates to John Tennent's *Epistle to Mead*, published in
1737. Bartholini's *Anatomica*, Vessalius' *De Humano Cor-
pore*, and Hopeman's *In Galen* were followed by Brown's
On the Muscles, Audry *On Worms*, Mead on *The Plague*
and Purcell *On Vapors*. Theories of fevers rubbed covers
with anatomies by Keil, Drake, and Chine. And crowning
all and copiously interleaved *The Poor Planter's Physician*
bulged out, at once the most worn and serviceable book
on the shelf. For with all the sagacious dignity of the
masters, Byrd turned to this volume when he wanted real
advice.

But, as was fitting, his most ample collection was in
literature. And what an anomaly it would have been for
an English visitor to walk into this library and find edi-
tions, most of them first, of all the significant authors of
his country. Here was Chaucer complete, and Edmund
Spenser, and, it would seem, nearly every Elizabethan
dramatist — Shakespeare, Ben Jonson, Beaumont and
Fletcher, Webster, Marlow, Ford, Shirley, Marston,
Chapman, and Dekker — represented in a ten-volume
collection. Thomas Browne's and Jeremy Taylor's works

were ranged beside those of the Puritan John Milton. And Restoration, Queen Anne, and contemporary authors had been assembled almost entire. Lee and Otway, Congreve, Cibber, and Byrd's old friend Wycherley stood out prominently, worn with much handling. Butler's *Hudibras* rested between the *Miscellanies* of Halifax and Shaftesbury's *Characteristics*; contempt for Puritans made them spiritually kin. The *Tale of a Tub* was grouped with Temple's *Letters*. The *Spectator Papers* and Dryden's works graced separate shelves. And further published works of Swift and of Mr. Pope gave the collection an indisputable modernity.

Then, when an inclination for tougher substance moved him, Byrd could read his law books or his classics. Aristotle and Sophocles were available in Greek, and in Latin, Horace, Cicero, Virgil, Lucretius, and Seneca. The Odyssey or Iliad might be read in French. And in this latter tongue he had an entire shelf of volumes, 'chiefly for entertainment,' which included everything from Rabelais, *L'amour des Dames*, and *Le Jésuit Défroqué*, to the stately tomes of Racine and Corneille.

Religious and philosophical treatises were not wanting. Byrd could mediate upon the quiet spirituality of Herbert's *Temple*, or he could peruse the *Leviathan* of Hobbes. In this thirty-six-hundred-volume collection, in short, he had brought to Virginia a library the like of which no other colonist before the Revolution ever managed to assemble. And it may almost be said that every line he wrote reflects in some degree his intimacy with the best thought and expression of the past.[8]

2

Times were not infrequent when Byrd, in his turn, left Westover for Williamsburg. His position as a veteran member of the Council required his presence there twice a year for purely professional reasons. Then there were always other more engaging if less urgent social inducements that brought him over, often with his family, on visits to friends.

General Court session at the capital was invariably an event long anticipated and prepared for. Mrs. de Graffenreid and Mrs. Stagg would have announced their 'Assemblies' as far as two months in advance. And there were professional male instructors also who vied with these two ladies in teaching the gallants of Virginia the terpsichorean graces of the Old World. Now, in 1737, William Dering had followed William Livingston by 'opening his school at the college, where all gentlemen's sons may be taught dancing, according to the newest French manner.' [9] And John Kello's ungallant remark about the young gentlemen and ladies of Hampton, Virginia, that, in their dancing, 'they discover great want of taste, and seldom appear with the grace and ease which these movements are calculated to supply,' surely had no application at all to society at the capital.

Byrd led a busy life when he went to Williamsburg on court days. There were nearly always two or three death sentences to be passed, for highway robbery or for the murder of illegitimate children. Less serious offenses demanded appropriate justice: public nuisances had to sit in the stocks or to be ducked, or thieves to be burnt in the hand.

But one invariably took a turn at the Fair, when judicial duties were over. Twice a year, in April and early December, this institution was held, 'with the laudable design to encourage trade.' And prizes would be given those bringing in for sale the greatest number of horses, cattle, sheep, or hogs.[10]

Always there were sports of the more communal sort accompanying the event: 'A hunting saddle with fine broadcloth housing' would be run for by 'any number of horses and mares.' A 'fine Cremona fiddle' would be played for by 'a number of county fiddlers'; a 'quire of ballads' would 'be sung for by a number of songsters, all of them to have liquor sufficient to clear their windpipes, and divers other prizes for dancing, football, jumping and wrestling,' would follow.[11]

Then there would be a jewelry lottery to attend. And a quite impressive one it was, announced formally in the *Gazette* as long as four months before:

Proposals

For the sale of sundry valuable jewels and plates, amounting to 400 pistoles, by way of lottery, for which there will be 400 tickets at a pistole [$3.80] each, eighty of which will be prizes; so that there will be four blanks to one prize. The lowest prize will be double the value of the ticket.

The greatest prize is to be one large brilliant diamond ring, set in diamonds, amethyst, three garnets, four emeralds, and nine rose diamonds.[12]

In these late spring or autumn afternoons, when the fair had grown dull and when lotteries were over, Byrd would attend Mrs. de Graffenreid's or Mrs. Stagg's Assemblies.

Everyone of importance would be there: Governor Gooch, leading Burgesses, his fellow Councillors, the Carters, the Lees, the Randolphs, John Custis, William and Mary students and faculty members. There was no place like this for mingling with the socially elect, unless, perhaps, it was the Raleigh Tavern.

One might stay at this inn as late as one desired. And it is probable that, when Byrd was in town without his family, he did remain there with other visiting friends until a tardy hour. The place was not so extravagantly gay as was the rule in Jefferson's time, nor had the capital itself quite earned the title he gave it, of 'Devilsburg.' The inn was patronized more exclusively by men, and unless a dance were following one of the Assemblies of the rival widow entertainers, or unless some Restoration play were being put on by amateurs of the town, there was no other place to spend an evening.

But Byrd went there by choice, because he wanted thoughtful companionship. It was a large wooden, two-storied structure, with a leaden bust of Sir Walter over the front door. Its main room was 'The Apollo,' meaning, one remembered, a 'banqueting-room,' such as Lucullus had had in his stately villa. It was well-lit, with a deep fire-place in the center, and carved wainscoting ornamented the space beneath the windows and above the mantel. 'Hilaritas sapientiae et bonae vitae proles,' advised a con-spicuous inscription above the hearth.[13] And Byrd, sipping his claret or port before the crackling blaze, nodded as he read it in philosophic acquiescence. It was a wise saying of a wise man. He could easily fancy having written it himself.

3

Thus the days passed for this gracious man, growing old now with genial friends, surrounded in his stately home with mellowing memories of England. But before his lawn at occasional intervals the ships would pass on their way to London, and leave him lonely, desiring. He would remember again his brave talk of ten years before, about a pilgrimage to Virginia and how it soon would be over. Futility was in the wind that fanned his face and swelled the white sails growing smaller in the distance. And he would walk back into his house in bitterness, because of a debt that would not be thrown off, for all his planning, and scheming, and prayer.

XII

USURER'S THRALL

Perhaps he even thought of going back once more, of flinging a last triumphant defiance at the bitter destiny which had chained him for so long. But more important considerations swept these braver ones away. After all, they were but the dreams of age, and had come too late.

I

An HUMBLE human being might have borne with reasonable composure the disappointments that seemed to mass themselves about Byrd during the last twelve years of his life. A man less born and trained to command would have effected a compromise, for, after all, they were of the pettiest sort. A few thousand pounds' indebtedness to a creditor, who, though importunate, lived across the Atlantic, was hardly a thing that should harass one's spirit for long hours, causing a man to lose his patience and dignity.

But all Byrd's interests had tended to make of him an individual who loved few things as he loved his liberty. To be obliged to another financially was 'to live in that hell to which all debtors are subject.' Well introduced through the industry and position of a father, he had on the whole found that life was good. His earlier reverses never seemed to touch, even approximately, the bottom of things. At most, they merely buffeted his pride. But by his sixtieth year this pride had become very greatly a part of him, and to wound it was to wound his innermost nature.

Yet Byrd the aristocrat found himself, at a period when

it was too late to make fresh starts, brought face to face
with this despicable question of money. There amid the
delights of his books, the peace and comparative con-
tentment of his Westover mansion, peered the ugly face
of the reality that he had for so long managed to avoid.
He became an innocent protagonist, suffering because of a
long past generosity. Now, too, he was old. It must have
seemed at times that some vast Malignity was at work
about him, undoing the just, ordered machinations of his
Deity. He may even upon occasions have doubted the
wisdom of a devotion to such unremunerative virtues as
integrity at all.

The blatant injustice of the whole business was so apparent! Why could not an old man who had worked well,
been fair and honest with his fellows, worshiped a gentleman's God with a true gentleman's dignity, and acted
always in a high-minded manner, spend the last of his days
in England, if he wished it, among the friends he most
cherished? Why was it, after living upon comparative
equality with these same friends, that he must burden his
letters to them now with entreaties for help, casting aside
as a sort of pretense all his former tacit implications of
wealth?

And why, more particularly, should the damned shade
of Daniel Parke, now twenty years murdered, plague him
through the persistence of a will, that document whose
unknown responsibilities he had assumed as a youth, in a
moment of gracious affection? These were no doubt insistent questions with Byrd, as he went about grasping at
this plan and that in hopes of escaping from 'the gripe of
an usurer.'

The details of his obligations to Micajah Perry, his London creditor, and the gradual steps in their settlement, are mostly beyond determination. One has seen that in 1723 he was aware of the debt's being considerably in excess of the amount first named to him, that he had already paid out one thousand pounds in addition to this sum, and that he vigorously renounced all further personal liability. For a long time thereafter the matter seems to have been settled. In 1728, Byrd wrote Perry in a decidedly intimate tone. He discussed European politics, 'the peevish humour of the Spaniards,' in particular; ordered from him six pairs of fisherman's boots, and closed with a courteous wish in behalf of Mrs. Perry's 'health and happiness.' [1] Evidently there had been no recent mention of money.

By 1733, it is equally evident that there had. The Alderman, as Byrd called his creditor, 'has published my engagements to him to all the world.' He writes a friend that he is endeavoring 'to get out of his clutches as soon as I can.' [2] Two years later he is 'selling off land and negroes to stay the stomach of that hungry magistrate.' The debt, however much it was, had been reduced by one thousand pounds in that interval.

Yet the business of working constantly, straining one's self to the utmost, was beginning to seem futile. There were other quite as honorable ways of making money. 'Can nothing be done for an old friend of forty years' acquaintance,' he wrote Sir Charles Wager, first lord of the Admiralty, 'to help him at this dead lift? I wish I could persuade you to take a little upon my account by speaking a good word for me to your friend Sir Robert Walpole. I have now taken my degrees for a small government, having served his Majesty as one of his Council full thirty years, and 'tis a little reasonable, after being so long a sharer in all the trouble of the government, to come at last to taste the profit of it.' [3] Byrd was asking for the position of Lieutenant-Governor, whose salary would have been adequate for his needs. But Wager gave him no help.

He busied himself elsewhere. He was anxious to get out of his difficulties in a grand manner. Finding the North Carolina Governor still prone to question his title to the Land of Eden, Byrd decided upon the pretentious idea of inducing the Virginia Assembly to grant him a vast one-hundred-thousand-acre tract on the south branch of Roanoke River and of bringing over a great number of Swiss emigrants to settle on both properties. He gave his fellow Councillors his assurance that he anticipated the early arrival of this colony, and they allowed him the territory, free of all taxes for two years, upon condition that within the interval he would settle 'one family at least upon every one thousand acres.' [4] He informed the insistent Carolina Governor that these people, who would 'guard the frontier and also lead the way in several useful improvements,' were monthly expected.[5] Byrd, of course, intended selling this property to them. His price was three pounds per hundred acres.[6] He had managed to increase his claims at Eden to twenty-six thousand acres, and a little later obtained an additional five thousand on the Roanoke. It gave him 131,000 acres for sale at this rate — more than four thousand pounds, if he could persuade these 'foreign Protestants' to come over! It was well worth trying.

He began a fervent correspondence with a Mr. Ochs,

who was about to bring to America a boatload of Swiss —
just the thing for his North Carolina holdings. The foothills were not far beyond, Byrd explained, 'and the
French are greatly anxious to make themselves masters
of all the mines with which there is reason to believe these
mountains abound.' The Indians tell absorbing stories
about silver being abundant there, 'and this is the more
probable because the mountains in the back of Virginia
and Carolina lie in the same parallel with those of New
Mexico.' It will be a simple matter for Ochs's colony 'to
engross all the trade with the Western Indians for skins
and furs.'

Byrd thinks the government will soon pass a law exempting settlers upon such frontier property as his own
of all taxes for a period of ten years. Meanwhile, one may
plant vineyards there, flax, hemp, silk grass, sugar, 'any
grain you please,' and fruit of every sort. 'The water,' he
declares, using a battered figure, 'is as clear as crystal and
sweet as milk.' Quarries of marble lie upon the hills. 'In
one word, there is nothing not deserving the name I have
given it of the Land of Eden.'

'I had much rather have to do with the honest Switzers,'
he adds, 'than the mixed people that come from Pennsylvania, especially when they are to be conducted by so
prudent a person as yourself.' [7]

But the 'Switzers' didn't come, for all his inviting word
pictures. Byrd was ready to give up. Soon the two years
would expire, and his land would lapse to the government.
His title to the Carolina property was not yet clear.
Preferment seemed out of the question. Why not sell
Westover and leave Virginia entirely? With its recently

completed mansion, the place should bring a good price, all his obligations could be wiped out, and he could spend his old age somewhere in a quiet, inexpensive place in a milder climate. Now that returning to London appeared out of the question, peace was the thing he most desired.

He offered the estate to Mr. Freeman, a wealthy friend of one of Daniel Parke's kinsmen. Freeman showed no interest. He next began making certain overtures to Mr. Peter Beckford, of Jamaica. 'I must emancipate myself,' he explained, 'from that slavery to which all debtors are subject.' This elderly gentleman was reputedly of vast wealth, and Byrd had known him for years. 'I have sent you as perfect a description of Westover as truth would permit me,' he wrote. 'I represented it honestly, as it is, and used not the French liberty of dressing it up as it ought to be.' [8]

He goes on to explain that he is enclosing a map of the place, a little rough, perhaps, 'but if it should not be found according to Art, it will make amends by being according to Truth.' If Beckford does not care to live in Virginia himself, why not buy the place for one of his sons? 'You can make a prince of him for less money here than you can make him a private gentleman in England.' Consider the blessings of the country! The Governor cannot oppress us, the negroes are neither so numerous nor so enterprising as to give us any apprehension, and we all lie securely with our doors unbarred, and can travel the whole country over without either arms or guard. 'And all of this,' he hastens to add, 'is not for want of money, but because we have no great city to shelter the thief, or pawnbroker to receive what he steals.'

A few weeks later, Byrd wrote Mrs. Pitt, of Bermuda, asking about the price of land there. His offer to Beckford had been so extremely attractive that it seemed only natural to think it would be accepted, with a considerable cash payment — a rare form of currency — into the bargain. 'I beg, Madam,' he requested to Mrs. Pitt, 'that you will be pleased to let me know how much a good share of land will sell for in sterling money, and how dear building is, and what would be the best commodity to send thither from this country.'⁹

He attributed his desire to leave Virginia to its bitter winters, condemning that climate he had so frequently praised to others who would further his interests by settling there. 'I should be glad if my affairs would give me leave to move with the birds of passage, a little more southerly when the cold weather approaches.' Not that his 'natural heat' had begun to decay. Byrd would never confess so distressing a thing to any lady. 'I was always subject to a cough,' he explained, 'and every winter I have more or less of my barking return upon me.'

Yet all these pleasant plans of spending his last days in the Summer Isles were contingent upon an old friend's purchasing Westover. And Beckford died before the offer reached him.

The death of Beckford seemed to cut off his only opportunity of escape. But now in this time of sore need a new hope sprang up from England. It appears that by the terms of Mrs. Byrd's father's will, the property this gentleman left his widow was to pass into the hands of the children, should she remarry. About 1735, this event actually happened. Madam Emmet, Byrd calls her, set-

tled down with her new husband. Prospects brightened.
Otway was surfeited with army life. He wanted to retire
to the country somewhere, and naturally Byrd needed his
wife's part of the fortune as never before. But meanwhile
Madam Emmet, through devious subtleties best known
to women, had got hold of all the legal papers involved in
the case and refused to part with them. The best Otway
could do was to secure a minor fraction of the inheritance,
which he promptly, and quite agreeably to Byrd, invested
in the Chelsea Water Works. This amount was so negligible a portion of what was due them that Byrd realized
his wife's share as being quite too small to meet his
present needs.

He harbored grave suspicions anent his mother-in-law's
good nature. 'Certainly,' he wrote a trustee, 'there is
something more than female obstinacy in her refusing to
deliver up the papers. There seems to be, besides, some
management betwixt her and Mr. Justice Farwell, and
were it not a little undutiful, I should mistrust our mother
to be in the plot.' If this be so, he adds, 'I hope the Lord
Chancellor will send her ladyship to the Fleet for her contempt.' [10] He expressed a further, more tenuous wish that
the executors would soon find a way to circumvent their
difficulties and somehow succeed in raising the money.
He was willing to dispose of Mrs. Byrd's interests now for
two thousand pounds. 'Would it be hard,' he asks, 'to
persuade some wealthy person to lay down this sum and
take the assignment of her fortune?'

His anxiety on this point was justified. 'The Alderman,'
he wrote Otway the same year, 'grows very clamorous' for
his money, notwithstanding he has the modesty to take

five per cent, and Byrd would be glad 'to stop his mouth' with the sum that was due his wife. 'This would stay his stomach,' he adds, 'and a little time would enable me to balance his account, which I should esteem a jubilee indeed, and the rather because it would enable me to make you a visit, which I long for of all things in the world.' [11]

But help was not forthcoming from this quarter either. After months of futile relying upon law courts, Byrd and Otway abandoned all idea of profiting from the estate until after Madam Emmet's death. And as late as 1741 it seemed to both of them as though her constitution were truly 'of English oak, and proof against all apoplexies as well as dropsies.' [12]

Yet in 1736, Byrd was not so convinced of his mother-in-law's hardihood. She suffered frequent attacks of one sort or another, would be prostrate for days, and while slowly convalescing often appeared a sweet, kindly disposed old lady — symptoms which to Byrd were proof conclusive that she was 'not long of this world.' Accordingly, he set to work upon other matters, hoping, quite unfilially, that each month would bring the comforting news of Madam Emmet's celestial translation.

Again he tried to get an appointment. Wager refused to recommend him for the governorship, but surely he would help in securing a much less pretentious office. 'I am going to entreat a favor of you,' Byrd wrote, 'which if granted would disentangle me from all my difficulties and make me perfectly easy. Mr. Phenny, the late surveyor of customs for the south district, is dead. The place he had is worth five hundred pounds a year and not unpleasant in the execution. If, therefore, by your credit with Sir Robert Walpole you would be pleased to get it for an old friend, 'twould make him happy in his declining years.' [13] But Wager was either too busy to help or indisposed even to try.

Still he persevered. Ochs's colony of Switzers had failed him, but he would attempt to persuade another. He went so far as to reconcile himself to the idea of settling Scotch-Irish upon his property. They were flocking over to America in such numbers 'that there is not elbow room for them,' swarming 'like the Goths and Vandals of old.' After all, though he personally disliked them, if they would buy his property at three pounds a hundred acres, that meant a major question disposed of.

The conclusion to his second experience with the Swiss was tragic, indeed. A shipload of these unfortunate immigrants, two hundred and fifty in number, left Europe with the intention of taking up one third of his Roanoke property. They sailed in the depth of winter, were four months at sea, and when they sighted land such a storm was raging that the vessel, 'either by the villany or stupidity of the master,' was wrecked on the coast. All the 'gentlemen of fortune' who were leading them, and most of the colony, perished. 'Some few of these unhappy wretches,' Byrd wrote a friend, 'are gone upon my land to make a beginning,' but their possessions were strewn upon the beach and, for the most part, destroyed.[14]

There was now nothing left to do but wheedle a band of Scotch-Irish into coming down from Pennsylvania. Byrd wrote his friend, the botanist Bartram, who had recently visited him from that colony, for assistance. He sent the letter by one of the Swiss gentlemen who had escaped the wreck and was bound for Philadelphia. He recounted his price, stressed the advantages of spending one's days in Virginia, exalted the Assembly's recent generosity in exempting foreign Protestants from their first ten years' taxes, and dwelt at great length upon the proximity of his Roanoke land to a good ship landing.

But Bartram was much too absorbed in his work to devote any attention to the colonizing business. When he visited the Old Dominion, two years before, and was directed to Westover to see Byrd's garden, he seems to have been disappointed. He was a Quaker, and a brother had advised him upon leaving Pennsylvania that 'though I should not esteem thee the less to come to me in what dress thou wilt, yet these Virginians are a very gentle, well-dressed people and look perhaps more on a man's outside than his inside. For these reasons please go clean, neat and handsomely dressed to Virginia.' [15]

It was for similar reasons that 'the father of American Botany,' a scientist in the strict sense of the term, felt in general that these Virginians were dabblers, interested in too many affairs at once, lacking the constant devotion to a calling that a true discipleship appeared to demand. He ignored Byrd's request.

He next wrote a Mr. Campbell at Norfolk, in hopes of getting his Scotchmen from a different source. Campbell was managing a large number of settlers, but he directed them to Carolina. 'It is a pity,' Byrd could not avoid telling him, 'that your Argyle clan makes their first trip to Cape Fear, where both the climate and the soil are worse than at Roanoke. Besides, in Carolina there is nothing but paper money, and that depending on a fund so precarious that the value is perpetually sinking. At Roanoke there is a healthy climate, a fruitful soil, with plenty of fish and fowl, and that will be a great ease to the newcomers.' [16] Yet these disclosures did not alter the fact that the newcomers went where they were told. It had begun to seem as though failure was inevitably the end of all his plans.

But he had to have money. For the first time in his experience, life was closing in on him, pressing him. He began selling land in small parcels; fifty acres here, a hundred there. He borrowed money on others of his plantations, 'and Maria, wife of said Byrd, relinquished her right of dower to land in said deed conveyed.' [17] Such a disagreeable business it was, obligating one's self to this friend and that: the Randolphs, Henry Cary, John Pleasants, William Cheatham, Samuel Tsheffely — even to strangers of quite an ordinary stripe. The loss of these properties lessened his revenue. He appeared in a sort of race with the Grim Reckoner, at times wondering whether he would not, for all his feverish desire, be the loser. And how vaguely unreal an illusion it must have seemed — this fancy, cherished long ago when he sailed from London, that his coming to Virginia would be only a necessary, soon ended 'pilgrimage to the new world.'

2

Exclusive of his Councillor duties, Byrd served only once in a public capacity after his work as dividing-line commissioner. In 1735, 'without reverencing the snow

that begins to whiten my head,' the King appointed him
as one of the three Crown representatives to determine the
true bounds of the Northern Neck. Comprising that
country between the headwaters of the Rappahannock
and Potomac Rivers, in what may roughly be called north-
west Virginia, that vast tract had all finally become vested
in the person of Thomas, Lord Fairfax. Originally, it consisted of several separate grants issued by Charles II,
while still an exile, to certain of his favorites. A long controversy had been raging as to the true source of these two
rivers. The adjustment of this dispute was the specific
objective of Byrd's commission.[18]

Fairfax at first generously agreed to submit to the report
of the royal surveyors. But later he grew apprehensive
and declared that with so much at stake he would by no
means leave the settlement of the controversy to any outside group whatever.[19] He appointed two assistants and,
with himself as a third member, formed a rival commission. Certain preliminary correspondence thereupon ensued between the two parties, before they formally severed
all relations.

They wrangled about the time of the year to start work.
Fairfax preferred spring. Byrd complained that snakes
were too bad then and insisted upon the fall. He also demanded that the other group meet his at the capital, Williamsburg. Williamsburg was objected to as being out
of the way. Mutual accusations of unfairness followed:
Fairfax's men had already begun the survey. They were,
for their own selfish interests, measuring one of the two
branches of the Rappahannock from water's edge to
water's edge, the other from bank to bank. Fairfax re-

joined by declaring that Byrd was willfully delaying the business by quibblings about a meeting-place.

Byrd would stand no more. He asserted that this last charge amounted to an insult, and that unless it was immediately substantiated or an apology offered, he would proceed in the matter alone. He had his commission, as he had had it before in North Carolina, and he meant to exercise it.

But in Fairfax, he had met his equal. This young lord appealed immediately to Attorney-General Barradale, who gave as his opinion that 'the King's commissioners had assumed a superiority in no ways becoming them.' [20] After obtaining this endorsement of his proceedings, Fairfax wrote his assistants to go ahead and make a separate map. He then, through Barradale, informed Byrd that he was willing to meet his party at the desired place, Williamsburg, if Byrd would guarantee that he meant no further delay. Such a preposterous request, from a man who had no official commission at all, Byrd of course completely ignored.

The two surveying bodies worked independently throughout. Byrd made his report in 1736 and sent it to England. It was obvious, he pointed out, that the land in question had been given out 'very much in the dark.' Between the time of the grant itself and the time of Fairfax's claiming the full extent of it, other settlers had moved into the disputed territory. This young lord insisted upon holding as his own a tract which, if all his titles were allowed, would amount to 5,282,000 acres. Even to a landed proprietor of Byrd's proportions, such arrogance was inconceivable. But inconceivable or no, when the other side submitted its report and both had been examined, His Majesty's decision was in favor of Fairfax.

3

During the last four years of his life, Byrd became intensely loyal to the mother country. His patriotism took the form of an inveterate hatred of the Spanish. How he wanted them driven from America, especially from Florida, where their presence created a constant menace to English supremacy! Now, in 1740, the British were planning to attack St. Augustine. Heart and soul he was for it! 'Everyone that lives on the northern continent must be convinced of the importance of the enterprise,' he wrote Lieutenant-Governor Gooch, 'and I wish that Virginia may have the honor of a share in it.' [21] To Wager, still first lord of the Admiralty, he communicated his grand scheme for expelling these abominable Catholics from the new world entirely. 'I have no great opinion of embarking landmen on such distant expeditions,' he declared. 'They will all be down with the scurvy and something like the gaol distemper by being stowed so thick on board.' Seamen will do much better, for they have a spirit and vigor beyond any landmen in those hot countries.

And instead of attacking Havana, 'it would be happier and more feasible to proclaim independence to all the Spanish West Indies and keep a sufficient force in those parts to protect them in it.' [22] The inhabitants of these colonies would be glad to throw off the tedious yoke their viceroys and governors have put upon them. 'Thus a free trade might be opened with those fine countries.'

The question of trade was the immediate cause of his anxiety. By a previous *assiento*, the English had agreed to shun all direct traffic with Spanish ports, excepting one ship only that was permitted to call at Porto Bello each year. But they managed to circumvent this restriction. The single large vessel would be followed by a fleet of smaller ones which would nightly carry off the goods stored upon it during the day. 'Other British smuggling vessels, pretending distress, would claim the right by treaty to enter Spanish harbors in the Gulf of Mexico. The colonial commerce of Spain was almost annihilated. In former days the tonnage of the fleet of Cadiz had amounted to fifteen thousand tons. It was now reduced to two thousand tons, and had no office but to carry the royal revenues from America.' [23] A considerable part of the population of Jamaica was sustained by the profits of this contraband industry. Still the mercantile interests of England clamored for war because, as has been aptly said, 'their traders were not allowed to smuggle with impunity.' [24]

Byrd had already written Walpole his opinion as to the more general policies the ministry should pursue. 'By reading over the history of England,' he observed, 'I find we never made war at a less expense or with greater advantage than when we stand upon our own legs and trust altogether to our wooden walls.' And certainly no better time than now for such a procedure could possibly be forthcoming, for England's strength vastly exceeded that of the enemy. 'A great superiority at sea,' he insists, 'will secure us from invasion and at the same time enable us to insult the enemy's coast and interrupt its fleets. It is to the interest of Great Britain to decide all her disputes upon her own element, and leave the people on the continent to fight their own battles.' At most, he concluded with considerable foresight, 'all we can get from the affectation of holding the balance of power in Europe is the honor of throwing into the light scale as much of our own substance as will bring the beam to the level.' [25]

4

The least of the distinctions that might have come to Byrd was long postponed. That rugged old Scotchman Blair, the same who almost half a century before had first undone him at the Lambeth Conference, refused, it seemed, to die. Gooch had been sent away to combat the Spaniards, and the government was left to the eldest member of the Council. That member was Blair, now nearly ninety years old. 'The country is a little dissatisfied with being governed by an ecclesiastic,' Byrd told Otway, 'the rather because of his great age and infirmity.' He was deaf and unable to sit in the Supreme Court. 'This I am forced to do in his stead, while he now and then nods in his chair.' [26] Blair died in 1743, but the presidency of the Council then had lost its glamour. It was like coming to a place of honor somehow by a back door.

The debt that had oppressed Byrd for so long was probably discharged in 1743. By the summer of 1740 he had reduced it to one thousand pounds. He tried to borrow that amount from Wager, but the attempt was unsuccessful. Besides, by this time it had become familiar — this owing one's fellow-man, this bargaining, trading, shifting to make ends meet. The world about him must have appeared a shallow, ill-adjusted, pretending thing in these last sympathyless years. For with all his dignity, affluence, and, especially, with all his vast extending properties — some 179,000 acres — he could not, without becoming a kind of slave himself, accomplish the task of effacing a debt — a task that should have amounted in truth to but 'a petty enterprise of small enforce.'

Perhaps, when he at last found himself free of this long-suffered burden, he turned again in memory to that England of his youth — an England where he had first known honor, and friendships that, though dimmed now, were yet able to warm his heart when he recalled them. Life had been rich there, rich in a way that the new world never quite seemed able to understand, or willing to concern itself about. Perhaps he even thought of going back once more, of flinging a last triumphant defiance at the bitter destiny which had chained him for so long. But more important considerations swept these braver ones away. After all, they were but the dreams of age, and had come too late.

Byrd died the twenty-sixth of August, 1744. They buried him in the garden, beside his daughter, amid the seemingly unending stillness of summer at Westover.

Someone, at a reasonably later date, caused the following to be carved on his monument:

Being born to one of the amplest fortunes in this country,
He was early sent to England for his education,
Where under the care and direction of Sir Robert Southwell,
And ever favored with his particular instructions,
He made a happy proficiency in polite and varied learning.

By the means of this same noble friend,
He was introduced to the acquaintance of many of the first per-
    sons of his age
For knowledge, wit, virtue, birth, of high station,
And particularly contracted a most intimate and bosom friend-
    ship
With the learned and illustrious Charles Boyle, Earl of Orrery.
He was called to the bar in the Middle Temple,
Studied for some time in the Low Countries,
Visited the Court of France,
And was chosen Fellow of the Royal Society.
Thus eminently fitted for the service and ornament of his coun-
    try,
He was made Receiver-General of His Majesty's revenues here,
Was thrice appointed public agent to the Court and Ministry of
    England,
And being thirty-seven years a member,
At last became President of the Council of that Colony.
To all this were added a great elegance of taste and life,
The well-bred gentleman and polite companion,
The splendid economist and prudent father of a family,
With the constant enemy of all exorbitant power,
And hearty friend to the liberties of his country.

THE END

SALEM COLLEGE LIBRARY
Winston-Salem, North Carolina

NOTES

I

1. J. S. Bassett, *Writings of Colonel William Byrd*, p. xvi.
2. Mrs. Gaskell, *Charlotte Brontë*, p. 37.
3. *Virginia Magazine of History and Biography*, XXXV (1927), 224.
4. *Ibid.*, XXXV (1927), 226.
5. *Ibid.*, XXXV (1927), 227.
6. J. S. Bassett, *op. cit.*, p. xliv.
7. *Virginia Historical Register*, I, 81.
8. *Virginia Magazine of History and Biography*, XXV (1927), 230.
9. From genealogy prepared by W. G. Stanard for *Beau Monde* and published by Bassett, *op. cit.* The spelling in this genealogy is revised in accordance with that submitted by the College of Heralds and loaned me through the courtesy of Mr. William Byrd, of New York City.
10. Mildred C. Whitaker, *Genealogy*, p. 86 ff.
11. *Virginia Magazine of History and Biography*, XXXV (1927), 229.
12. J. S. Bassett, *op. cit.*, p. xvi.
13. *Virginia Magazine of History and Biography*, XXXV (1927), 227.
14. John Fiske, *Old Virginia and Her Neighbours*, II, 65.
15. G. L. Beer, *The Old Colonial System*, II, 139.
16. Sainsbury, *Abstracts*, XVI, 101.
17. The Byrds were never revolutionists. Mrs. William Byrd III, a sister of Benedict Arnold's wife, entertained Cornwallis and officers of his army most elegantly at Westover in 1781. *Virginia Magazine of History and Biography*, XXXVIII (1930), 1–40.
18. 'Mrs. Byrd's Relation,' *Eggleston Transcripts*, pp. 28–30.
19. Byrd to Lane and Perry, 5–10–1686. *Virginia Historical Register*, I, 350.
20. J. S. Bassett, *op. cit.*, p. xix.
21. *Ibid.*
22. P. A. Bruce, *Institutional History of Virginia in the Seventeenth Century*, I, 350.
23. Hening, *Statutes*, II, 517.
24. Bassett, *op. cit.*, p. xx.
25. He was a member of the Royal Society for forty-eight years, receiving its publications annually.
26. Byrd to Frank Otway, 1740. *Virginia Magazine of History and Biography*, XXXVII (1929), 33.

II

1. Byrd was admitted April 12, 1692. E. A. Jones, *American Members of the Inns of Court*, p. 35.
2. Jesse, *London*, II, 297.
3. *Ibid.*, II, 288.
4. *King Henry the Sixth* (Part First), II, 4.
5. Preface to 1741 edition, I, x. This account probably survives as the engaging introduction to the *History of the Line.*
6. R. R. Pearce, *A History of the Inns of Court*, p. 388.
7. *Ibid.*, p. 393.
8. Jesse, *op. cit.*, II, 288.
9. R. R. Pearce, *op. cit.*, p. 396.
10. *Ibid.*, p. 81.
11. *Ibid.*, p. 128.
12. *Virginia Magazine of History and Biography*, IX (1901), 241.
13. *Patrician and Plebeian in Virginia*, p. 3.
14. A complete auditing of his books was then conducted, at the request of the Lords of Trade, by Byrd II; see his *To Facetia by Veramour*, Appendix.
15. P. A. Bruce, *Social Life in Virginia in the Seventeenth Century*, p. 203.
16. Hening, *Statutes*, III, 205.
17. See Palmer, *Calendar of Virginia State Papers*, I, 213; 218–19.
18. Mary N. Stanard, *op. cit.*, p. 344.
19. Ann Maury, *Memoirs of a Huguenot Family*, p. 267.
20. J. S. Bassett, *op. cit.*, p. xlv.
21. J. E. Cooke, *Virginia*, p. 305.
22. L. G. Tyler, *Williamsburg*, p. 119.
23. *Ibid.*, p. 118.
24. W. S. Perry, *Papers Relating to the Church in Virginia*, I, 36–64. This volume contains a *verbatim* report of the conference.
25. This, however, was not the sole reason for Andros's recall.
26. E. A. Jones, *op. cit.*, p. 35.
27. J. S. Bassett, *op. cit.*, Introduction, xlv.
28. R. A. Brock, *Huguenot Emigration to Virginia*, p. 15.
29. Sainsbury, *Abstracts*, II, 179.
30. John Fiske, *Old Virginia and Her Neighbours*, p. 205.
31. Sainsbury, *op. cit.*, II, 186.
32. Council *Minutes*, I, 316–17.
33. *Journal of the House of Burgesses*, III, 313–16.
34. Sainsbury, *Abstracts*, II, 329.
35. *Journal of the House of Burgesses*, III, xliii.

36. Sainsbury, *op. cit.*, II, 338.
37. *Ibid.*, II, 259.
38. *Ibid.*, II, 274.
39. *Ibid.*, II, 301.
40. W. G. Stanard and Mary Stanard, *The Colonial Virginia Register*, p. 6.

III

1. Byrd, *To Facetia*, p. 2. The late Thomas Fortune Ryan, about 1914, had published privately fifteen copies of these letters and, it is believed, distributed them among his friends. The copy I have used — the property of the Virginia Historical Society — was made available through the courtesy of its secretary, Mr. W. G. Stanard. It is an attractive quarto of some thirty-two pages. A scholarly and well-written appendix contains identifications of many of the characters mentioned, though nothing is said of the historical Facetia. The letters are introduced by another paper of Byrd's 'Observations on the Place of Auditor.' An effort to discover how Ryan got hold of the letters, or whom he employed as editor of the book, has been entirely fruitless.
2. Sir Roger (1675–1739), third baronet of a distinguished Welsh family, was an hereditary Tory who had supported Daniel Finch, second Earl of Nottingham, and won his daughter, a celebrated beauty. He was an ardent opponent of Walpole's excise bill in 1733.
3. Byrd, *To Facetia*, Appendix III.
4. *Ibid.*, p. 11.
5. Thomas Wharton, fifth Baron Wharton (1658?–1715). One of a race famous for beauty, ability, and lack of morals, he was brought up in strictest puritanism, but had hardly entered upon his career before his abandoned profligacy 'astounded all Europe.' He married and neglected Anne, daughter of Sir Henry Lee, fifth Baronet of Ditchley, who brought him ten thousand pounds dowry and twenty-five hundred pounds per year, out of which he maintained, among other things, the greatest racing stud in Europe. He was a vehement Whig and Protestant and among the first to join William of Orange, and composed the song 'Lilliburlo,' set to music by Purcell, that, as he boasted, 'sang a king out of three kingdoms.' Swift hated him, satirized him as 'Verres,' and described him as 'wholly occupied with vice and politics.' For his second wife he married Lucy, daughter of Viscount Lisburne, a woman as abandoned as himself and to whose infidelities he was cynically indifferent. He died at his home in Dover Street in April,

1715. 'The most universal villain I ever knew,' writes a contemporary.

6. *To Facetia*, p. 16.

7. *Ibid.*, p. 26.

8. *Ibid.*, p. 29.

9. John Ashton, *Social Life in the Reign of Queen Anne*, p. 191.

10. Byrd, *To Facetia*, Appendix VIII.

11. *Ibid.*, p. 30.

12. This duel between Wharton (cf. note 5) and the son of his old friend, Sir Thomas Dashwood, took place on the second of September, 1703. Dashwood the elder was almost as conspicuous a debauchee as Wharton himself, and at one time president of the Hell Fire Club, of which both were worthy members. *Ibid.*, Appendix X.

13. See catalogue of the library in *The Writings of Colonel William Byrd of Westover* (Bassett ed.), p. 413 ff.

14. *To Facetia*, p. 20.

15. W. J. Courthope, *Addison*, p. 90.

16. For February 27, 1698–99.

17. W. J. Courthope, *op. cit.*, p. 103.

18. See also his 'Ode to the Memory of Mrs. Killigrew.'

19. W. J. Courthope, *op. cit.*, p. 103.

20. The other two theaters of Anne's reign were Dorset Gardens and Lincoln's Inn Fields.

21. John Ashton, *op. cit.*, p. 353.

22. *Ibid.*

23. *Spectator* No. 240.

24. *Ibid.*

25. *To Facetia*, p. 31. Perhaps it was worry over her husband's belligerent temperament that hastened her death. Jack was constantly taking exception to the slightest remarks, if they questioned her ability. 'Damme!' he would say, peeling off his coat, 'though I don't much value my wife, yet nobody shall affront her, by God!'

26. H. D. Traill, *Social England*, IV, 395.

27. J. Ashton, *op. cit.*, p. 270.

28. *Spectator* No. 18.

29. J. S. Bassett, *The Writings of Colonel William Byrd*, p. xxxix.

30. *Ibid.*

31. *Virginia Magazine of History and Biography*, XXXV (1927), 238.

32. *Ibid.*, 234.

IV

1. See his letter to Gooch. *Virginia Magazine of History and Biography*, XXXVII (1927), 101 ff.
2. John Fiske, *Old Virginia and Her Neighbours*, p. 245.
3. By Edmund Ruffin, Petersburg, as Appendix IX to the *Farmer's Register*. Another two-volume edition was published by Thomas Wynne, Richmond, 1866. The best has been done by Bassett for Doubleday, Page, New York, 1901. Mark Van Doren edited the most recent edition for Macy-Masius, New York, 1928.
4. *Social Life in the Reign of Queen Anne*, p. 280.
5. *Virginia Magazine of History and Biography*, XXXVI (1928), 212. (Letters to Spotswood, 12–30–35.)
6. John Ashton, *op. cit.*, p. 317.
7. J. S. Bassett, *op. cit.*, p. xlvii.
8. *William and Mary Quarterly*, I (1921), 186.
9. *Ibid.*, 189.
10. *Ibid.*, 190.
11. He never spells the word twice in the same way.
12. *Ibid.*, 194.
13. Sainsbury, *Abstracts*, VI, 316.
14. J. S. Bassett, *op. cit.*, p. xliv.
15. 'Observations on the Place of Auditor,' *To Facetia*, p. 4.
16. *Ibid.*, p. 6 ff.
17. Byrd, *Title Book*, p. 195. (Virginia Historical Society MSS.)
18. L. G. Tyler, *Williamsburg*, p. 125.
19. J. S. Bassett, *op. cit.*, p. 1.
20. Mary Stanard, *Colonial Virginia*, p. 172.
21. *Ibid.*, p. 166.
22. *A Progress to the Mines* (Bassett's ed.), p. 339.
23. *Ibid.*, p. 338.
24. J. S. Bassett, *op. cit.*, p. xliv.
25. P. A. Bruce, *Institutional History of Virginia*, II, 358.
26. *Ibid.*, II, 360.
27. *Ibid.*, II, 361.
28. P. A. Bruce, *Social Life in Virginia*, p. 137.
29. *Ibid.*, p. 140.
30. W. N. Sainsbury, *Abstracts*, III, 661.
31. Bruce, *Institutional History of Virginia*, p. 137.
32. *Ibid.*
33. *Ibid.*, II, 361.
34. Sainsbury, *Abstracts*, XVIII, 51.
35. *Ibid.*, XVIII, 78, 110.

36. Bruce, *Institutional History of Virginia*, II, 362.
37. Robert Beverley, *History of Virginia*, p. 390.
38. *Ibid.*, p. 226.
39. *Ibid.*
40. T. J. Wertenbaker, *Patrician and Plebeian in Virginia*, pp. 97–98.
41. *Ibid.*
42. Sainsbury, *Abstracts*, IX, 132.
43. M. D. Conway, *Barons of the Potomack and Rappahannock*, p. 213.

V

1. Blair's estimate of him. *Virginia Magazine of History and Biography*, XX (1912), 373.
2. Byrd, *Title Book*, p. 85.
3. A copy of the will appears in the *Virginia Magazine of History and Biography*, XX (1912), 373 ff.
4. *Ibid.*, XX (1912), 380.
5. P. A. Bruce, *Economic History of Virginia*, II, 259.
6. *Valentine Papers*, II, 1402.
7. *Virginia Magazine of History and Biography*, XXXVI (1928), 213. (Letter to Otway, 1736.)
8. *Virginia Magazine of History and Biography*, XXXV (1927), 377–78.
9. *Ibid.*
10. This act is found in Hening, *Statutes*, IV, 29.
11. Sainsbury, *Abstracts*, VIII, 377.
12. See page 107.
13. *Virginia Magazine of History and Biography*, XX (1912), 380.
14. J. S. Bassett, *op. cit.*, p. li.
15. *Ibid.*, p. lx.
16. *Virginia Magazine of History and Biography*, XXXV (1927), 380. (Letter to Custis, 2–4–1711.)
17. *Ibid.*, XXXV (1927), 382. (Letter to Custis, 2–7–1711.)
18. *Ibid.*, XXXVI (1928), 38. (Letter to Custis, 7–29–1723.)
19. Council *Minutes*, I, 507.
20. *Ibid.*, I, 516.
21. Palmer, *Calendar of Virginia State Papers*, I, 152.
22. *Ibid.*, I, 154.
23. *Ibid.*, I, 155–60.
24. Sainsbury, *Abstracts*, VIII, 385.
25. Palmer, *op. cit.*, I, 170.
26. *Ibid.*, I, 16.
27. Council *Minutes*, I, 558.

28. Spotswood, *Official Letters*, II, 86.
29. *Ibid.*, II, 117.
30. Sainsbury, *Abstracts*, III, 453.
31. *Ibid.*, III, 456.
32. *Ibid.*, III, 478.
33. *Ibid.*, III, 616, 630.
34. Bassett, *op. cit.*, p. lxiii.
35. Custis, *Recollections of Washington*, p. 6.; quoted in Bassett, *op. cit.*, p. lxxv.

VI

1. Hening, *Statutes*, III, 288.
2. *Ibid.*, III, 178.
3. W. E. Ford, *The Controversy Between Spotswood and his Council*, p. 9.
4. Sainsbury, *Abstracts*, III, 524.
5. J. S. Bassett, *op. cit.*, p. lxix.
6. Spotswood, *Official Letters*, II, 260.
7. Quoted in Bassett, *op. cit.*, p. lxx.
8. Palmer, *Calendar of Virginia State Papers*, I, 190–93.
9. W. C. Ford, *op. cit.*, p. 23.
10. Sainsbury, *Abstracts*, III, 678.
11. *Ibid.*, III, 691.
12. Council *Minutes* for this date. Taken from Bassett, *op. cit.*, p. lxxii.
13. *Ibid.*, December 9, 1718.
14. Letter of May 15, 1719. Bassett, *op. cit.*, p. lxxiii.
15. Sainsbury, *Abstracts*, III, 712.
16. *Ibid.*, III, 725.
17. Spotswood, *Official Letters*, II, 304.
18. Sainsbury, *op. cit.*, III, 753.
19. *Ibid.*, III, 741.
20. *Ibid.*, III, 759.
21. *Ibid.*, III, 766.
22. Palmer, *Calendar of Virginia State Papers*, I, 195.
23. Sainsbury, *Abstracts*, III, 809.
24. *Journal of the House of Burgesses*, V, 229.
25. Council *Journal*, II, 657.
26. *Journal of the House of Burgesses*, V, 310.
27. *Ibid.*

VII

1. *Virginia Magazine of History and Biography*, XXXV (1927), 383. (Letter to Charmante, 10–23–1722.)
2. *Ibid.*
3. *Ibid.*, XXXV (1927), 384. (Letter to Charmante, 10–26–1722.)
4. *Ibid.*, XXXV (1927), 385.
5. *Ibid.*, XXXV (1927), 386.
6. *Ibid.* (Letter of 10–30–1722.)
7. *Ibid.*, XXXV (1927), 387–88.
8. *Ibid.*, XXXV (1927), 388, note.
9. Constance C. Harrison, 'Colonel William Byrd of Westover,' *Century* XLII (1891), 171.
10. *Ibid.*
11. *Henry Esmond*, p. 147.
12. Quoted by Constance C. Harrison, *op. cit.*, 172.
13. *Ibid.*, 170.
14. *Orrery Papers*, I, 52. (Letter of 2–2–1726–27.)
15. *Ibid.*, I, 59. (Letter of 2–3–1727–28.)
16. *Virginia Gazette*, December 2, 1737.
17. *Virginia Magazine of History and Biography*, XXXVI (1928), 37. (Letter of 7–29–1723.)
18. *Ibid.*, XXXV (1927), 375. The date was May 9, 1724.
19. Constance C. Harrison, *op. cit.*, 172
20. *Virginia Magazine of History and Biography*, XXXVI (1928), 119.
21. *Ibid.*, XXXVI (1928), 222. (Letter to Lord Egmont, 7–12–1736.)
22. *Ibid.*, XXXVI (1928), 37. (See the letter to Custis, 7–29–23.)
23. *Orrery Papers*, I, 118. (Letter to Orrery, 1732.)
24. Ann Maury, *Memoirs of a Huguenot Family*, p. 249.
25. In 1723. Aspinwall, *Transcripts*, p. 8.
26. *Ibid.*
27. T. J. Wertenbaker, *The Planters of Colonial Virginia*, p. 126.
28. *Ibid.*, p. 136.
29. Hening, *Statutes*, IV, 354.
30. Meade, *Old Churches and Families of Virginia*, I, 190.
31. H. Howe, *Historical Collections of Virginia*, p. 331.
32. Mary N. Stanard, *Colonial Virginia*, p. 229.
33. L. G. Tyler, *Williamsburg*, p. 230.
34. Tyler, *op. cit.*, p. 264.

VIII

1. *Orrery Papers*, I, 49.
2. *Ibid.*, I, 50.

3. *Ibid.*, I, 52.
4. *Ibid.*
5. *Ibid.*, I, 54.
6. W. K. Boyd, *William Byrd's Dividing Line Histories*, Introduction, p. xvii.
7. *The Present State of Virginia*, p. 111.
8. *Ibid.*, p. 96.
9. See Boyd, *op. cit.* (Introduction), for complete history of the question.
10. See their commission in Bassett, *op. cit.*, p. 267 ff.
11. Byrd, *Secret History*, p. 21.
12. See Bassett, *op. cit.*, p. 268.
13. Byrd, *Secret History*, p. 59.
14. *Ibid.*
15. *Ibid.*, p. 63.
16. *Ibid.*, p. 81.
17. *Ibid.*, p. 93.
18. *Ibid.*, p. 99.
19. *Ibid.*, p. xxii, Introduction.
20. *Ibid.*, p. 169.
21. *Ibid.*
22. *Ibid.*, p. xxiii. The defenses of both parties appear in full in Bassett, *op. cit.*, p. 271 ff.
23. *Ibid.*, p. 171.
24. *Ibid.*, p. 174.
25. *Ibid.*
26. *Ibid.*, p. 185.
27. *Ibid.*, p. 186.
28. Sainsbury, *Abstracts*, IX, 475.
29. *Virginia Magazine of History and Biography*, IX (1901), 125.
30. E. G. Swem, *Description of the Dismal with a Proposal to Drain*, p. 21.
31. *Virginia Magazine of History and Biography*, XXXVI (1928), 114. (Letter to Bladen, 7–1728.)
32. Swem, *op. cit.*, p. 28.
33. *Ibid.*, p. 30.

IX

1. Edited by Boyd, *op. cit.*
2. *Virginia Magazine of History and Biography*, XXXVI (1928), 355. (Letter to Collinson, 7–18–1736.)
3. Bassett, *op. cit.*, p. lxxix.
4. Byrd, *History of the Dividing Line*, p. 19. (Bassett's ed.)

5. See Boyd's excellent introduction upon which the following discussion is in part based.
6. *Ibid.*, p. xiv.
7. Byrd, *History of the Dividing Line*, p. 5. (Bassett's ed.)
8. *Ibid.*, p. 37.
9. *Ibid.*, p. 78.
10. *Ibid.*, p. 48.
11. *Ibid., History of the Dividing Line*, p. 44.
12. *Ibid.*, p. 46.
13. *Ibid.*, p. 75.
14. *Ibid.*, p. 60.
15. *Ibid.*, p. 126.
16. *Ibid.*, p. 128.
17. *Ibid.*, p. 96.
18. *Ibid.*, p. 103.
19. *Ibid.*, p. 99.
20. *Ibid.*, p. 101.
21. *Ibid.*, p. 140 ff.
22. *Ibid.*, p. 145.
23. *Ibid.*, p. 83.
24. *Ibid.*, p. 251.
25. *Ibid.*, p. 198.
26. *Ibid.*, p. 190.

X

1. Byrd, *A Progress to the Mines*, p. 333. (Bassett's ed.)
2. *Ibid.*, p. 337.
3. *Ibid.*, p. 340.
4. *Ibid.*, p. 342.
5. *Ibid.*, p. 348.
6. *Ibid.*, p. 358.
7. *Ibid.*, p. 361.
8. *Ibid.*, p. 366.
9. *Ibid.*, p. 372.
10. *Ibid.*, p. 383.
11. Byrd, *A Journey to Eden*, p. 284. (Bassett's ed.)
12. *Ibid.*, p. 287.
13. *Virginia Gazette* (April 22, 29; May 6, 1737).
14. Byrd, *op. cit.*, p. 299.
15. *Ibid.*, p. 300.
16. *Ibid.*, p. 305.
17. *Virginia Magazine of History and Biography*, XXXVI (1928), 220-21. (Byrd to Egmont, 7-12-36.)

18. *Virginia Magazine of History and Biography*, XXXVI (1928), 220–21. (Byrd to Egmont, 7–12–36), p. 311.
19. *Ibid.*, p. 314.
20. *Ibid.*, p. 317.
21. *Ibid.*, p. 321.
22. *Ibid.*, p. 325.

XI

1. Edith T. Sale, *Manors of Virginia*, p. 137.
2. *Virginia Magazine of History and Biography*, XXXVII (1929), 113. (Mrs. Taylor to Byrd, 1–18–42.)
3. *Ibid.*, 115.
4. *Ibid.*, XXXVI (1928), 266. (Letter to Mrs. Otway, 6–30–36.)
5. *Ibid.*, IX (1901), 239.
6. Quoted in Bassett, *op. cit.*, pp. 399–400.
7. *Ibid.*, p. 400 (note).
8. For a complete catalogue of the library see *ibid.*, p. 413 ff. (Appendix A.)
9. *Virginia Gazette*, 11–18–37.
10. *Ibid.*, 12–7–39.
11. *Ibid.*, 11–19–36.
12. *Ibid.*, 7–22–39.
13. 'Mirth is the offspring of wisdom and a good life.'

XII

1. *Virginia Magazine of History and Biography*, XXXVI (1928), 42. (Letter to Perry, 7–28–1728.)
2. *Ibid.*, IX (1901), 125. (Letter, 8–20–1733.)
3. *Ibid.*, p. 126.
4. Palmer, *Calendar*, I, 233.
5. *Virginia Magazine of History and Biography*, IX (1901), 127. (Letter to Johnson, 5–23–1735.)
6. *William and Mary Quarterly*, VI (1926), 313. (Letter to Bartram, 3–23–1739.)
7. *Virginia Magazine of History and Biography*, IX (1901), 225. (Letter to Ochs, 1726.)
8. *Ibid.*, XXXVI (1928), 122. (Letter to Beckford, 12–6–1735.)
9. *Ibid.*, IX (1901), 237. (Letter to Mrs. Pitt, 1–6–1736.)
10. *Ibid.*, 247. (Letter to Pratt, 6–24–1736.)
11. *Ibid.*, XXXVI (1928), 213. (Fragment of letter to Otway, 1736.)
12. *Ibid.*, XXXVII (1929), 28. (Letter to Otway, 2–1741.)
13. *Ibid.*, XXXVI (1928), 359. (Letter to Wager, 1737.)

Vol II, 265 pages. (First exact printing of the Westover manuscripts.)

Byrd, William: *The Writings of Colonel William Byrd*, New York, 1901, Doubleday, Page Co. Editor, John Spencer Bassett. lxxxviii, 461 pages.

Byrd, William: *Letters Writ to Facetia by Veramour*, 1703. Baltimore, 1913, The Munder Press. 38 pages. (Fifteen copies privately printed for Thomas Fortune Ryan, Esq.)

Byrd, William: *Description of the Dismal Swamp and a Proposal to Drain the Swamp*. 1728–36. Metuchen, N.J., 1922, Earl G. Swen, editor. 32 pages. Charles F. Heartman, printer.

Byrd, William: *Letters*. (In addition to several of the above sources they are to be found in *The Virginia Magazine*, IX (1901), XXXV (1927), XXXVI (1928), XXXVII (1929); *William and Mary Quarterly*, I (1921); *Orrery Papers*.)

Case of the Planters of Tobacco in Virginia, The, As represented by themselves; to which is added *A Vindication of the Said Representation*. London, 1733, J. Roberts, printer. 64 pages.

Chandler, J. A. C., and Thames, T. B.: *Colonial Virginia*, Richmond, 1907, Times Dispatch Co. 386 pages.

Calendar of Virginia State Papers and Other Manuscripts. 1652–1781. Richmond, 1875, ed. Wm. P. Palmer. 2 vols. (used Vol. I, 613 pages), R. F. Walker.

Conway, Moncure D.: *Barons of the Potomack and the Rappahannock*, New York, 1892, The Grolier Club. 290 pages.

Cook, Elizabeth C.: *Literary Influences in Colonial Newspapers*, 1704–50. New York, 1912, Columbia University Press. 279 pages.

Cooke, John Esten: *Virginia*, Boston, 1903, Houghton Mifflin. 521 pages.

Courthope, W. J.: *Addison*, New York, 1903, Macmillan. 197 pages. (E.M.L.S.)

Cunningham, Peter: *Handbook for London*, London, 1849, John Murray. 2 volumes. 933 pages.

Davies, Samuel: *The Curse of Cowardice, a Sermon Preached to the Militia of Hanover County*. 1758. London, 1758, J. Buckland. 36 pages.

Documents Relating to the Huguenot Emigration to Virginia, Richmond, 1886. Ed. R. A. Brock. Virginia Historical Society, publishers. 247 pages.

Eggleston Transcripts. 'Bacon's Rebellion.' (Compiled by Rev. Edward Eggleston, 1886, being copies of Egerton MSS. 2395, British Museum.) MSS. Department, Virginia State Library.

Fiske, John: *Old Virginia and Her Neighbours*, Boston, 1897, Houghton Mifflin. 2 vols. (used Vol. II, 419 pages).

Force's Historical Tracts, II, 15. 'A Description of the Province of South Carolina,' Charleston, 1731. Reprinted by Peter Force, Washington, 1832.

Ford, W. C.: *The Controversy Between Lieutenant Governor Spotswood and his Council and the House of Burgesses on the Appointment of Judges on Commissions of Oyer and Terminer*, Brooklyn, 1891, The Historical Printing Club. 61 pages.

Gaines, Francis P.: *The Southern Plantation: a Study in the Development and the Accuracy of a Tradition*, New York, 1924, Columbia University Press. 243 pages.

Gaskell, Elizabeth C.: *The Life of Charlotte Brontë*, New York, 1873, Scribner, Welford Co. 452 pages.

Gooch Papers. Virginia Historical Society (copies from British Transcripts in Library of Congress). 3 vols., 1107 pages. Vol. I, 1727–31; Vol. II, 1732–40; Vol. III, 1741–51.

Hall, F.: *The Importance of the British Plantations in America to this Kingdom, as also a Description of Several of the Colonies There*, London, 1731. J. Peele, printer. 114 pages.

Harrison, Constance C.: 'Colonel William Byrd of Westover,' *Century Magazine*, 42 (1891), 163.

Hartwell, Blair, and Chilton: *The Present State of Virginia and the College*, London, 1727, John Wyat. 95 pages. (Written *circa* 1697.)

Hening, William W.: *The Statutes at Large, Being a Collection of all the Laws of Virginia*. 4 vols. Vols. I and II, New York, 1823, R. and W. and G. Bartow; Vol. III, Philadelphia, 1823, Thomas De Silver; Vol. IV, Richmond, 1820, W. W. Gray.

Holmes, George K.: *Tobacco Crop of the United States*, 1612–1911. Washington, 1912, Government Printing Office. 12 pages.

Howe, Henry: *Historical Collections of Virginia*, Charleston, S.C., 1845, Babcock & Co. 544 pages.

Jefferson, Thomas: *Notes on the State of Virginia*, Philadelphia, 1801, R. T. Rawle. 436 pages.

Jesse, J. H.: *London and Its Celebrities*, London, 1850, Richard Bentley. 2 vols. (used Vol. II). 479 pages.

James, E. A.: *American Members of the Inns of Court*, London, 1924, W. D. Smith & Son (The St. Catherine Press). 250 pages.

Jones, Hugh: *The Present State of Virginia*, London, 1724, J. Clark (Sabien Reprints). 151 pages.

Journals of the House of Burgesses of Virginia, Ed. H. R. McIlwaine, Richmond, 1912–13. 5 vols. Everett Waddy & Co. (The Colonial Press).

Keith, Sir William: *History of the British Plantations in America*, Part I, *A History of Virginia*. London, 1738, S. Richardson. 187 pages.

Lecky, W. E. H.: *A History of England in the Eighteenth Century*, New York, 1878, D. Appleton Co. 2 vols. (used Vol. I). 626 pages.

Legislative Journals of the Council of Colonial Virginia, Richmond, 1918, ed. H. R. McIlwaine. 3 vols. Everett Waddy & Co.

Letters Which Passed Between the Commissioners for Settling the Disputed Boundary of Northern Neck, 1736–37. MSS. (Virginia State Library), 19 letters. 10 pages.

Loftie, W. J.: *The Inns of Court and Chancery*, London, 1908, Seeley & Co. 302 pages.

Martin, Joseph: *A New and Comprehensive Gazeteer of Virginia*, Charlottesville, 1835. Mosely & Tompkins, 623 pages.

Maury, Ann: *Memoirs of a Huguenot Family* (from the autobiography of James Fontaine), New York, 1872, G. P. Putnam's Sons. 512 pages.

Meade, Bishop: *Old Churches, Ministers, and Families of Virginia*, Philadelphia, 1889, J. B. Lippincott Co. 2 vols. Vol. I, 490 pages; Vol. II, 496 pages.

Miller, Elmer I.: *The Legislature of the Province of Virginia*, New York, 1907, Columbia University Press. 182 pages.

Minutes of the Council and General Court of Colonial Virginia, ed. H. R. McIlwaine, Richmond, 1924, 2 vols., Everett Waddy Co.

McDonald, James J.: *Life in Old Virginia*, Norfolk, 1907, Old Virginia Publishing Co. 374 pages.

McIlwaine, H. R.: 'The Struggle for Religious Toleration in Virginia,' *Johns Hopkins Studies in Political Science*, XII (1894), 1–65.

Oldmixon, John: *The British Empire in America*, London, 1741, J. Brotherton. 2 vols. (used Vol. I). 567 pages.

Orrery Papers, London, 1903. Duckworth & Co., ed. Countess of Cork and Orrery. 2 vols. Vol. I, 321 pages; Vol II, 331 pages.

Pearce, R. R.: *History of the Inns of Court*, London, *circa* 1850.

Perry, William Stevens: *Papers Relating to the Church in Virginia* (privately printed, 1870), 1650–1776. 585 pages.

Pulling, Alexander: *The Order of the Coif*, Boston, 1897, Boston Book Co. 297 pages.

Poems on Several Occasions, by a gentleman of Virginia. Williamsburg, 1736. William Parks, 30 pages, ed. by E. G. Swem and reprinted by Charles F. Heartman, New York, 1920.

Reply to the Vindications of the Representation of the Case of the Planters of Tobacco in Virginia, London, 1733, R. Carlton, printer. 18 pages.

Ripley, William Z.: *The Financial History of Virginia*, 1609–1776, New York, 1893, Columbia Press. 170 pages.

Sainsbury Abstracts. Twenty volumes, manuscripts, in Virginia State Library. (Copies of titles and copious abstracts of all papers concerning Virginia found in London Public Record Office; transcribed by W. Noel Sainsbury, 1873.)

Saunders, William L.: *The Colonial Records of North Carolina*, II, 1713–28, Raleigh, 1886.

Sioussat, St. George L.: *Virginia and the English Commercial System*, 1730–1733. Washington, 1906, Government Printing Office. 97 pages.

Spotswood, A.: *The Official Letters of Alexander Spotswood*, Richmond, 1885, ed. R. A. Brock. 2 vols. Virginia Historical Society Publication.

Stanard, Mary N.: *Colonial Virginia, Its People and Customs*, Philadelphia, 1917, J. B. Lippincott & Co. 375 pages.

Stanard, William G. and Mary N.: *The Colonial Virginia Register*, Albany, N.Y., 1902, Joel Mansell Sons. 249 pages.

Stith, William: *The History of the First Discovery and Settlement of Virginia*, Williamsburg, 1747, William Parks. 331 pages. Reprinted for Joseph Sabin, N.Y., 1865.

Traill, H. D.: *Social England*, New York, 1905, G. P. Putnam's Sons. 6 vols. (used Vols. IV, V).

Tyler, Lyon G.: *Williamsburg, the Old Colonial Capital*, Richmond, 1907, Whitlet and Shepperson. 285 pages.

Valentine, E. P.: *The Edward Pleasants Valentine Papers*, Richmond, 1929, Whitlet and Shepperson. 4 vols. 2768 pages.

Virginia Magazine of History and Biography, Richmond, published quarterly since 1893, W. G. Stanard, ed., Virginia Historical Society.

Virginia Gazette, Williamsburg, 1736. Official and first Virginia newspaper. William Parks, publisher. (Files, 1736–38, in Virginia State Library and Virginia Historical Society; 1738–40, in Virginia Historical Society; 1745–46, in Virginia Historical Society — these the only files extant before 1750.)

Warren, Charles: *History of the American Bar*, Boston, 1911, Little, Brown & Co. 586 pages.

Wertenbaker, T. J.: *Patrician and Plebeian in Virginia*, Charlottesville, Va., 1910, The Michie Company. 239 pages.

Wertenbaker, T. J.: *The Planters of Colonial Virginia*, Princeton, 1922, Princeton University Press. 260 pages.

Whitaker, Mildred C.: *Genealogy of the Campbell, Noble, Gaston, Shelton, Gilmour, and Byrd Families*, St. Louis, 1927, The Mound City Press. 230 pages.

William and Mary College Quarterly, Williamsburg (published quarterly since 1921), eds. J. A. C. Chandler and E. G. Swem.

INDEX